W9-BEV-471

Houghton
Mifflin
Harcourt

Math

Grade 8

Printed in the U.S.A.

ISBN 978-0-544-26826-5

6 7 8 9 10   0928   22 21 20 19 18 17

4500647526   B C D E F G

Core Skills Math

GRADE 8

Table of Contents

© Houghton Mifflin Harcourt Publishing Company

Mathematics Correlation Chart

Skills	Page Numbers
Circles	117
Constructions	56, 57
Data Analysis	96, 97, 98, 99, 100, 101, 102, 103, 104
Exponents and Roots	1, 2, 3, 4, 5, 6, 7, 8, 9, 10
Fractions and Decimals	43, 44, 45, 46, 47, 48, 49, 118, 119
Interpreting and Analyzing Graphs	71, 72, 73
Linear Equations	74, 75, 76, 86, 87, 88, 89
Lines and Angles	51, 52, 53, 54, 55
Order of Operations	66
Probability	105, 106, 108, 109
Problem Solving	27, 50, 61, 70, 95, 107, 123
Properties	62, 63
Pythagorean Theorem	127, 128, 129, 130, 131, 132, 133, 134, 135, 136, 137
Ratio, Proportion, and Percent	58, 59, 60
Rational and Irrational Numbers	64, 65
Relations and Functions	67, 68, 69, 83, 84, 85
Scientific Notation	11, 12, 13, 14, 15
Similar and Congruent Figures	110, 111, 112, 113, 114, 115, 116
Slope	77, 78, 79, 80, 81, 82
Solid Geometry	120, 121, 122
Solving One-Variable Equations	16, 17, 18, 19, 20, 21, 22, 23, 24, 25, 26
Systems of Equations	90, 91, 92, 93, 94
Transformations	28, 29, 30, 31, 32, 33, 34, 35, 36, 37, 38, 39, 40, 41, 42
Triangles	124, 125, 126

Exploring Squares and Square Roots

1. Since 4 is the square root of 16 and 5 is the square root of 25, would you estimate $\sqrt{22}$ to be closer to 4 or to 5? Explain your answer.

   _____

2. Use a calculator. What is $\sqrt{22}$?

   _____

Use a calculator. Write the square or square root of each number in standard form.

3. 20^2 _____   4. 32^2 _____   5. 3.2^2 _____   6. 3.02^2 _____

7. $\sqrt{169}$ _____   8. $\sqrt{81}$ _____   9. $\sqrt{625}$ _____   10. $\sqrt{6.25}$ _____

11. $\sqrt{0.0625}$ _____   12. $\sqrt{484}$ _____   13. $\sqrt{4.84}$ _____   14. $\sqrt{256}$ _____

15. $\sqrt{2.56}$ _____   16. $\sqrt{0.0256}$ _____

MIXED REVIEW

Round to the place indicated.

17. $2.49

   ten cents _____

18. 21.23

   tenths _____

19. 45,638

   thousands _____

20. 745,831

   ten thousands _____

21. 68,974

   ten thousands _____

22. 682,401

   thousands _____

Tell which operation to perform first. Then solve.

23. $(16 \div 4) \times 2$ _____   24. $13 + 9 - 8$ _____

25. $20 \times (10 - 2)$ _____   26. $(8 \div 4) + 2 \times 6$ _____

27. $(40 - 6) \times 8$ _____   28. $81 \div (3 \times 3)$ _____

Name _____ Date _____

Irrational Numbers

Round each irrational number to the nearest hundredth.

1. $\sqrt{34}$

_____

2. $\sqrt{82}$

_____

3. $\sqrt{45}$

_____

4. $\sqrt{104}$

_____

5. $\sqrt{71}$

_____

6. $\sqrt{19}$

_____

7. $\sqrt{24}$

_____

8. $\sqrt{41}$

_____

9. $\sqrt{40}$

_____

10. $\sqrt{21}$

_____

11. $\sqrt{56}$

_____

12. $\sqrt{39}$

_____

13. $\sqrt{23}$

_____

14. $\sqrt{47}$

_____

15. $\sqrt{65}$

_____

16. $\sqrt{35}$

_____

17. $\sqrt{13}$

_____

18. $\sqrt{79}$

_____

19. $\sqrt{75}$

_____

20. $\sqrt{97}$

_____

21. $\sqrt{89}$

_____

22. $\sqrt{30}$

_____

23. $\sqrt{95}$

_____

24. $\sqrt{12}$

_____

25. $\sqrt{57}$

_____

Squares and Square Roots

Write *SR* if the first number is the square root of the second number, write *S* if it is the square, or write *N* if it is neither.

1. 9, 81   **2.** 15, 225   **3.** 169, 13   **4.** 125, 5   **5.** 2, 4

_____   _____   _____   _____   _____

Find the square of each number.

6. 3^2 **7.** 14^2 **8.** $(-7)^2$ **9.** $(-13)^2$ **10.** $(-16)^2$

_____   _____   _____   _____   _____

11. $(0.6)^2$ **12.** $\left(\dfrac{4}{5}\right)^2$ **13.** $\left(-\dfrac{5}{12}\right)^2$ **14.** $\left(\dfrac{13}{6}\right)^2$

_____   _____   _____   _____

Find the two square roots of each number.

15. 121   **16.** 256   **17.** 196   **18.** 400   **19.** 900

_____   _____   _____   _____   _____

Find each square root.

20. $\sqrt{49}$ **21.** $\sqrt{81}$ **22.** $\sqrt{144}$ **23.** $\sqrt{64}$ **24.** $\sqrt{225}$

_____   _____   _____   _____   _____

MIXED APPLICATIONS

25. The formula for the distance, *d*, an accelerating car can travel is $d = 5.6t^2$. How many minutes, *t*, does the car take to travel 1,814.4 m?

_____

26. The backyard of a house is a square whose area is 900 m². How much fencing is needed to enclose the yard?

_____

NUMBER SENSE

27. Bob was thinking of a number between 5 and 15 that when squared and added to 23 equals the next number's square. What is the number?

_____

Square Roots

Find each square or square root.

1. 15^2 _____   2. $\sqrt{64}$ _____   3. 10^2 _____   4. $-\sqrt{25}$ _____

5. $\left(\frac{1}{4}\right)^2$ _____   6. $\sqrt{196}$ _____   7. $(2.11)^2$ _____   8. $-\sqrt{1/121}$ _____

9. $\left(\frac{2}{9}\right)^2$ _____   10. $\sqrt{0.64}$ _____   11. $(-8)^2$ _____   12. $\sqrt{0.0036}$ _____

Estimate each square root to the nearest tenth.

13. $\sqrt{24}$ _____   14. $\sqrt{73}$ _____   15. $\sqrt{146}$ _____   16. $\sqrt{5}$ _____

17. $\sqrt{101}$ _____   18. $\sqrt{61}$ _____   19. $\sqrt{300}$ _____   20. $\sqrt{486}$ _____

Use a calculator to find each square root. Round to the nearest tenth.

21. $\sqrt{21}$ _____   22. $\sqrt{56}$ _____   23. $\sqrt{13}$ _____   24. $\sqrt{91}$ _____

25. $\sqrt{110}$ _____   26. $\sqrt{87}$ _____   27. $\sqrt{250}$ _____   28. $\sqrt{17}$ _____

MIXED APPLICATIONS

29. A square lot has an area of 160,000 square feet. What is the length of each side?

_____

30. A circle has a circumference of 35.2 cm. What is its diameter to the nearest tenth?

_____

31. What is the 6% sales tax on a computer that costs $4,200?

_____

32. A square room has a floor area of 410 m². What is the length of each side to the nearest tenth of a meter?

_____

NUMBER SENSE

33. You know that there are whole numbers between any two perfect squares greater than 0. Between which of these pairs of perfect squares are there more whole numbers? Answer without calculating. Circle *a* or *b*.

    a. between 59^2 and 60^2 **b.** between 590^2 and 591^2

4

Finding Square Roots

Estimate to find each square root to the nearest tenth.

1. $\sqrt{89}$ _____

2. $\sqrt{123}$ _____

3. $\sqrt{20}$ _____

4. $\sqrt{61}$ _____

Find each square root to the nearest hundredth.

5. $\sqrt{3}$ _____

6. $\sqrt{17}$ _____

7. $-\sqrt{34}$ _____

8. $\sqrt{87}$ _____

9. $\sqrt{124}$ _____

10. $\sqrt{111}$ _____

11. $\sqrt{0.04}$ _____

12. $-\sqrt{0.21}$ _____

Find the square root to the nearest tenth when $a = 7$ and $b = 2$.

13. $\sqrt{a - b}$ _____

14. $\sqrt{a^2}$ _____

15. $\sqrt{b^2 + a}$ _____

MIXED APPLICATIONS

Use the graph for Exercises 16–18. The graph shows the positive square roots of the numbers from 1 to 50.

16. What is the approximate square root of 50?

_____

17. What is the approximate square root of 30?

_____

18. Can you approximate the square root of 0.07? Explain.

_____

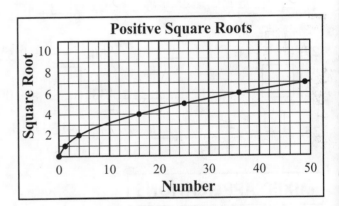

Positive Square Roots

WRITER'S CORNER

19. Give one advantage and one disadvantage of using a graph to find square roots.

_____

_____

_____

Powers and Exponents

Write each in exponent form.

1. $2 \times 2 \times 2$ _____

2. $5 \times 5 \times 5 \times 5$ _____

3. 6×6 _____

4. $4 \times 4 \times 4 \times 4$ _____

5. $7 \times 7 \times 7$ _____

6. 14×14 _____

7. $1 \times 1 \times 1 \times 1 \times 1$ _____

8. $10 \times 10 \times 10$ _____

9. $1.8 \times 1.8 \times 1.8 \times 1.8$ _____

Find each value. You may use your calculator.

10. 2^7 _____

11. 9^3 _____

12. 7^2 _____

13. 8^0 _____

14. 4^1 _____

15. 2^4 _____

16. 7^4 _____

17. 13^1 _____

18. 5^2 _____

19. 10^0 _____

20. 6^4 _____

21. 5^4 _____

22. 9^1 _____

23. 7^1 _____

24. 4^2 _____

25. 2^3 _____

Complete.

26. $2^{\square} = 16$ _____

27. $6^{\square} = 1$ _____

28. $\square^2 = 1$ _____

29. $4^{\square} = 1$ _____

30. $5^{\square} = 125$ _____

31. $4^{\square} = 16$ _____

32. $\square^4 = 6{,}561$ _____

33. $\square^5 = 100{,}000$ _____

34. $\square^2 = 25$ _____

35. $3^{\square} = 27$ _____

36. $27^{\square} = 27$ _____

37. $\square^2 = 169$ _____

MIXED APPLICATIONS

38. The formula for the volume of a cube is $V = s^3$ where V is the volume and s is the length of each side. Find the volume of a cube when the length of each side is 3.2 cm. Write the answer in cubic centimeters.

_____

39. Jack saved 2 pennies today. If he doubles the number of pennies he saves each day, how many more days will it take until he has saved more than 1,000 pennies?

_____

MIXED REVIEW

40. Round 8.8095 to the nearest tenth.

_____

41. Write the standard form of 1.2 million.

_____

Compare and Order

Compare. Write <, >, or =.

1. $\sqrt{3} + 2 \bigcirc \sqrt{2} + 3$

2. $\sqrt{11} + 15 \bigcirc \sqrt{15} + 11$

3. $\sqrt{6} + 5 \bigcirc 6 + \sqrt{5}$

4. $\sqrt{9} + 3 \bigcirc 9 + \sqrt{3}$

5. $\sqrt{15} - 3 \bigcirc -2 + \sqrt{5}$

6. $10 - \sqrt{8} \bigcirc 12 - \sqrt{2}$

7. $\sqrt{7} + 1 \bigcirc \sqrt{10} - 1$

8. $\sqrt{12} + 3 \bigcirc 3 + \sqrt{11}$

9. $\sqrt{14} + 5 \bigcirc \sqrt{16} + 9$

10. $2\sqrt{13} + 4\sqrt{17} \bigcirc \pi - 2\sqrt{2} + 5\sqrt{3}$

11. $5 + \sqrt{16} \bigcirc 10 - \sqrt{1}$

12. $(\sqrt{13} + 3) + \sqrt{12} \bigcirc \sqrt{13} + (3 + \sqrt{12})$

13. $-10 + \sqrt{4} \bigcirc \sqrt{5} + \sqrt{4}$

14. $\sqrt{25} + \sqrt{9} \bigcirc \sqrt{25} \div \sqrt{4}$

Order the numbers from least to greatest.

15. $\sqrt{4}, -\sqrt{4}, 4^2, (\sqrt{4})^3$

16. $\sqrt{25}, \pi, \sqrt{4}, \sqrt{2}, \sqrt{7}$

_____

_____

17. $\sqrt{7}, \pi, -\frac{1}{3}, \sqrt{11}$

18. $\pi, \sqrt{16}, \sqrt{7}, \sqrt{9}, 5$

_____

_____

19. $3.5, \pi, \sqrt{7}, 8, \sqrt{4}$

20. $\sqrt{2}, \sqrt{4}, \sqrt{13}, \pi, \sqrt{8}$

_____

_____

21. $4, \sqrt{36}, \frac{1}{3}, -\sqrt{49}$

22. $\sqrt{7}, \sqrt{\frac{7}{2}}, 2$

_____

_____

23. $\sqrt{10}, \pi, 3.5$

24. $1.5, \sqrt{\frac{12}{3}}, \sqrt{3}$

_____

_____

25. $2\sqrt{7}, \sqrt{24}, 2\pi$

_____

Name _____ Date _____

Exploring Exponents

Extend the pattern for the powers of 10.

1. $10^4 = 10,000$

$10^5 = 100,000$

$10^6 =$ _____

$10^7 =$ _____

2. $10^{-2} = 0.01$

$10^{-3} = 0.001$

$10^{-4} =$ _____

$10^{-5} =$ _____

Complete.

3. $3^3 = 3 \times 3 \times 3 = 27$

$3^2 =$ _____ = _____

$3^1 =$ _____ = _____

$3^0 =$ _____ = _____

4. $3^{-1} = \dfrac{1^1}{3} = \dfrac{1}{3}$

$3^{-2} =$ _____ = _____

$3^{-3} =$ _____ = _____

$3^{-4} =$ _____ = _____

Rewrite each fraction using a negative exponent.

5. $\left(\dfrac{1}{10}\right)^5$ _____

6. $\left(\dfrac{1}{3}\right)^9$ _____

7. $\left(\dfrac{1}{10}\right)^{11}$ _____

8. $\left(\dfrac{1}{6}\right)^3$ _____

Rewrite each expression using a positive exponent.

9. 10^{-9} _____

10. 2^{-14} _____

11. 4^{-8} _____

12. 10^{-12} _____

Write each number using a base of 10 and a negative exponent.

13. 0.00001 _____

14. 0.0000001 _____

MIXED REVIEW

The figures are similar. Find x.

15.

3 cm, 2 cm

x, 4 cm _____

16.

12 mm

12 mm

x

5 mm _____

Find each unit price.

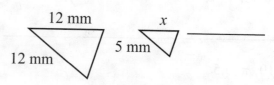

17. 8 for $2.56 _____

18. 25 for $14.00 _____

19. 6 for $13.14 _____

8

Integers as Exponents

Write as an expression having a negative exponent and using the least possible base value.

1. $\left(\frac{1}{5}\right)^1 =$ _____

2. $\left(\frac{1}{10}\right)^7 =$ _____

3. $\left(\frac{1}{8}\right)^3 =$ _____

4. $\frac{1}{100} =$ _____

5. $\frac{1}{2 \cdot 2 \cdot 2 \cdot 2 \cdot 2} =$ _____

6. $\frac{1}{64} =$ _____

7. $\frac{1}{27} =$ _____

8. $\frac{1}{1,000,000} =$ _____

9. $\frac{1}{25} =$ _____

Write as a fraction or as a decimal in simplest form.

10. $10^{-4} =$ _____

11. $10^{-7} =$ _____

12. $10^{-6} =$ _____

13. $2^{-5} =$ _____

14. $3^{-1} =$ _____

15. $10^{-1} =$ _____

16. $9^{-2} =$ _____

17. $5^{-3} =$ _____

18. $3^{-4} =$ _____

19. $10^{-2} =$ _____

20. $4^{-2} =$ _____

21. $11^{-2} =$ _____

22. $(-6)^{-1} =$ _____

23. $(-3)^{-3} =$ _____

24. $(-5)^{-2} =$ _____

25. $(-2)^{-6} =$ _____

26. $(-12)^{-1} =$ _____

27. $(-12)^{-2} =$ _____

MIXED APPLICATIONS

Tell whether you would use an expression with a positive exponent or an expression with a negative exponent for Exercises 28–29.

28. The weight of a dust particle is about 0.0000001 g.

29. Sound travels about 1,300,000 m per hour.

LOGICAL REASONING

30. Consider the numbers $9,999^{-1}$, $9,999^{-3}$, $9,999^{-4}$, and so on. Are any of these numbers negative? Explain your answer.

Core Skills Math, Grade 8

Name _____ Date _____

Exploring Products and Quotients of Powers

Write the addition or subtraction expression that will give you the exponent of each answer.

1. $9 \cdot 9^9$ _____

2. $10^4 \cdot 10^{-4}$ _____

3. $7^2 \div 7^{-3}$ _____

4. $4^{-9} \div 4^{-9}$ _____

5. $10^{-10} \div 10$ _____

6. $12^{-7} \div 12^{-2}$ _____

Write each product as one power.

7. $2^4 \cdot 2^6$ _____

8. $4^4 \cdot 4^5$ _____

9. $8^{10} \cdot 8$ _____

10. $14^{-7} \cdot 14$ _____

11. $9^{-5} \cdot 9^{-4}$ _____

12. $3^6 \cdot 3^{-5}$ _____

13. $7^{-10} \cdot 7^2$ _____

14. $6^8 \cdot 6^5$ _____

15. $(-10)^{-3} \cdot (-10)^8$ _____

16. $(-5)^4 \cdot (-5)^{-9}$ _____

17. $(-6)^{-4} \cdot (-6)^8 \cdot (-6)^{-5}$ _____

Write each quotient as one power.

18. $4^4 \div 4^3$ _____

19. $10^6 \div 10$ _____

20. $12^2 \div 12$ _____

21. $8^{12} \div 8^{10}$ _____

22. $9^3 \div 9^{-6}$ _____

23. $11^{-7} \div 11^5$ _____

24. $3^{-2} \div 3^{-3}$ _____

25. $10^{-5} \div 10^{-8}$ _____

26. $2^{-6} \div 2^6$ _____

27. $(-9)^0 \div (-9)^{-9}$ _____

28. $(-7)^{-10} \div (-7)^0$ _____

29. $(4.2)^{-3} \div (4.2)^{-2}$ _____

SCIENCE CONNECTION

30. Medical research develops new drugs to treat diseases. Much of the research takes place in pharmaceutical laboratories. Suppose a researcher tests a prototype antibiotic on a certain strain of bacteria. If the antibiotic kills the bacteria at a rate of 7^{15} bacteria per second, how many bacteria would be killed at 7^{10} seconds?

_____

_____

_____

10

Exploring Scientific Notation

Complete the following.

1. $0.000095 = 9.5 \times$ _____

2. $0.000836 = 8.36 \times$ _____

3. _____ $\times 10^{-3} = 0.00705$

4. _____ $\times 10^{-5} = 0.00002119$

Write in scientific notation.

5. 0.0000364 _____

6. 0.00751 _____

7. 0.10005 _____

8. $1,094$ _____

9. 0.00000099 _____

10. 0.04101 _____

11. $10,500$ _____

12. $8,900$ _____

Write in standard form.

13. 7.4×10^{-4} _____

14. 8.3×10^{-2} _____

15. 1.95×10^{-3} _____

16. 2.8×10^{-5} _____

17. 5.45×10^{3} _____

18. 9.2×10^{5} _____

19. 6.091×10^{-4} _____

20. 9.09×10^{-1} _____

MIXED APPLICATIONS

21. The speed of light is about 3×10^5 kilometers per second. Write this speed in standard form.

_____

22. How many seconds are there in one week? Write your answer in scientific notation.

_____

LOGICAL REASONING

23. Without writing these numbers in standard form, order them from least to greatest.

4.1×10^7 3.62×10^{-6} 4.1×10^{-2} 3.62×10^{-2} 4.1×10^9

_____

Scientific Notation

Express each number in standard form.

1. 5×10^2 _____

2. 1.45×10^5 _____

3. 6.072×10^6 _____

4. 4.8×10^{-3} _____

5. 7.41×10^{-5} _____

6. 1.9×10^{-4} _____

7. 3×10^8 _____

8. 7×10^9 _____

9. 2.6645×10^5 _____

10. 5.7832×10^{-3} _____

11. 7.62953×10^{-4} _____

12. 8.51×10^{12} _____

Express each number in scientific notation.

13. 4,100 _____

14. 0.0000054 _____

15. 9,920,000 _____

16. 0.008 _____

17. 70,500 _____

18. 0.000301 _____

19. 6,853,429,781 _____

20. 135,677 _____

21. 0.00088 _____

22. 1,246,912 _____

23. 0.00007629 _____

24. 564,372 _____

12

More Scientific Notation

Write in scientific notation.

1. 12,000 _____

2. 57,000,000,000 _____

3. 0.00043 _____

4. 0.00000000876 _____

5. 0.0024 _____

6. 0.00000017 _____

7. 0.000009 _____

8. 80,450,000 _____

9. 6,300,000,000 _____

10. 0.0000006 _____

Write in standard form.

11. 4×10^5 _____

12. 5.7×10^3 _____

13. 9×10^6 _____

14. 5×10^2 _____

15. 3.3×10^7 _____

16. 9×10^{-4} _____

17. 6.4×10^{-2} _____

18. 2.3×10^3 _____

19. 9×10^5 _____

20. 5×10^{-7} _____

MIXED APPLICATIONS

21. The diameter of a thin wire is 0.0000067 m. Write the number in scientific notation.

_____

22. The number of rice seeds in a bag is 385,000,000. Write this number in word form.

_____

_____

SCIENCE CONNECTION

23. Much biological research involves breeding plants. A research scientist estimates that a certain hybrid plant produces 12,500,000 grains of pollen and that the grains are 0.00092 in. long. Write these numbers in scientific notation.

_____

13

Operations with Scientific Notation

Add or subtract. Write each answer in scientific notation.

1. $2.35 \times 10^8 + 4.61 \times 10^8$ _____

2. $5.83 \times 10^5 + 1.45 \times 10^5$ _____

3. $5.84 \times 10^8 + 2.64 \times 10^7$ _____

4. $3.76 \times 10^{12} + 5.21 \times 10^{13}$ _____

5. $7.43 \times 10^7 + 5.21 \times 10^9$ _____

6. $4.3 \times 10^6 - 3.26 \times 10^6$ _____

7. $6.49 \times 10^3 - 3.97 \times 10^3$ _____

8. $8.91 \times 10^{13} - 3.87 \times 10^{12}$ _____

9. $6.38 \times 10^7 - 7.45 \times 10^5$ _____

10. $3.2 \times 10^5 + 4.9 \times 10^8$ _____

11. $4.378 \times 10^{12} + 7.701 \times 10^7$ _____

12. $2.3 \times 10^8 - 2.12 \times 10^3$ _____

13. $4.55 \times 10^{15} - 7.4 \times 10^{11}$ _____

14. $6.35 \times 10^3 + 1.65 \times 10^6$ _____

15. $5 \times 10^3 - 1.23 \times 10^2$ _____

Multiply or divide. Write each answer in scientific notation.

16. $(4.4 \times 10^6) \times (3.9 \times 10^4)$ _____

17. $(2.8 \times 10^8) \times (1.9 \times 10^4)$ _____

18. $(1.3 \times 10^9) \times (4.7 \times 10^5)$ _____

19. $(3.7 \times 10^{15}) \times (5.2 \times 10^7)$ _____

20. $(4.9 \times 10^{24}) \times (1.6 \times 10^5)$ _____

21. $(5.76 \times 10^9) \div (3.2 \times 10^3)$ _____

22. $(3.72 \times 10^8) \div (1.2 \times 10^5)$ _____

23. $(3.6 \times 10^4) \div (6 \times 10^5)$ _____

24. $(1.44 \times 10^{24}) \div (1.2 \times 10^{17})$ _____

25. $(1.8 \times 10^9)(6.78 \times 10^{12})$ _____

26. $(5.092 \times 10^{21})(3.38 \times 10^6)$ _____

27. $\dfrac{8.4 \times 10^{21}}{4.2 \times 10^{14}}$ _____

28. $\dfrac{3.46 \times 10^{17}}{2 \times 10^9}$ _____

Apply Scientific Notation

1. A newborn baby has about 26,000,000,000 cells. An adult has about 1.9×10^3 times as many cells as a newborn. About how many cells does an adult have? Write your answer in scientific notation.

   _____

2. The edge of a cube measures 3.5×10^{-2} meters. What is the volume of the cube in cubic meters? Write your answer in scientific notation.

   _____

3. The smallest state in the United States is Rhode Island, with a land area of about 2.9×10^{10} square feet. The largest state is Alaska, whose land area is about 5.5×10^2 as great as the land area of Rhode Island. What is the land area of Alaska in square feet? Write your answer in scientific notation.

   _____

4. Astronomers estimate that the diameter of the Andromeda galaxy is approximately 2.2×10^5 light-years. A light-year is the distance light travels in a vacuum in 1 year. One light-year is approximately 5.9×10^{12} miles. What is the diameter of the Andromeda galaxy in miles? Write your answer in scientific notation.

   _____

The table below shows the approximate populations of three countries.

Country	China	France	Australia
Population	1.33×10^9	6.48×10^7	2.15×10^7

5. How many more people live in France than in Australia? Write your answer in scientific notation.

   _____

6. The area of Australia is about 2.95×10^6 square miles. What is the approximate average number of people per square mile in Australia?

   _____

7. What is the ratio of the population of China to the population of France? What does this mean?

   _____

Name _____ Date _____

Equations with Squares and Cubes

Solve.

1. $a^2 = 25$ _____

2. $x^3 = 729$ _____

3. $c^2 = 4$ _____

4. $t^2 = 169$ _____

5. $l^3 = 216$ _____

6. $y^3 = 8$ _____

7. $p^2 = 36$ _____

8. $t^2 = 16$ _____

9. $s^3 = 1,331$ _____

10. $v^2 = 81$ _____

11. $b^3 = 3,375$ _____

12. $g^3 = 512$ _____

13. $x^2 = 9$ _____

14. $b^3 = 1$ _____

15. $w^2 = 256$ _____

16. $p^3 = 4,096$ _____

17. $s^2 = 100$ _____

18. $q^3 = 64$ _____

19. $z^2 = 1$ _____

20. $w^3 = 27$ _____

21. $k^2 = 49$ _____

22. $o^3 = 125$ _____

23. $j^2 = 121$ _____

24. $h^3 = 343$ _____

25. $m^2 = 64$ _____

26. $m^3 = 1,000$ _____

27. $u^2 = 144$ _____

28. $g^3 = 2,197$ _____

29. $a^2 = 225$ _____

30. $e^3 = 2,744$ _____

31. $k^2 = 196$ _____

32. $r^3 = 1,728$ _____

MIXED REVIEW

Solve each equation. Check your solutions.

33. $u + 26 = 73$ _____

34. $z - 115 = 247$ _____

35. $4n = 104$ _____

36. $\frac{x}{8} = 56$ _____

Write the prime factorization of each number using exponents.

37. 24 _____

38. 32 _____

39. 116 _____

Subtraction Equations

Solve each equation. Check your solutions.

1. $m - 6 = 32$

2. $k - 53 = 24$

3. $z - 40 = 35$

4. $w - 17 = 67$

_____ _____ _____ _____

5. $53 = g - 15$

6. $t - 5.7 = 5.7$

7. $1.2 = s - 4.9$

8. $(9 + 12) = r - 8$

_____ _____ _____ _____

Choose a variable and tell what it represents. Then write an equation for each word sentence.

9. Ten fewer than the number of band instruments is 47 instruments.

10. The number of meters decreased by 25.6 is 84.3 meters.

_____ _____

MIXED APPLICATIONS

For Exercises 11–12, write an equation or equations. Then solve.

11. Fred paid $248 for a business suit. This was $55 less than the regular price of the suit. What was the regular price of the suit?

12. Mike's age, decreased by the age of his 4-year-old sister, is 11. Mike's age, increased by his uncle's age, is 53. How old is Mike's uncle?

_____ _____

MIXED REVIEW

Compute.

13. $2 + 7 \times 8$

14. $4^2 + (21 - 15)$

15. $7 + 13 \div 13 - 4$

16. $(18 - 5) - 3 \times 4$

_____ _____ _____ _____

Solve each equation.

17. $x + 8 = 29$

18. $63 = 16 + c$

19. $4.5 = y + 2.8$

20. $z + 40 = 40$

_____ _____ _____ _____

Core Skills Math, Grade 8

Multiplication Equations

Solve each equation. Check your solutions.

1. $7n = 56$

_____

2. $2x = 94$

_____

3. $6q = 312$

_____

4. $2.7r = 8.1$

_____

5. $12t = 180$

_____

6. $8s = 1,000$

_____

7. $25p = 260$

_____

8. $700 = 35b$

_____

9. $1.8k = 7.2$

_____

10. $0.6m = 30$

_____

11. $0.7j = 0.42$

_____

12. $4.5y = 18$

_____

13. $5s = 615$

_____

14. $0.4a = 9.44$

_____

15. $51.6 = 2c$

_____

16. $602 = 7k$

_____

17. $43e = 1,376$

_____

18. $9.1h = 3.64$

_____

19. $8n = 43$

_____

20. $4t = (1.5 \times 8)$

_____

MIXED APPLICATIONS

Write an equation. Then solve.

21. June owes a balance of $1,308.24 on a car loan. She has 9 more equal monthly payments to make. How much is each monthly payment?

_____

22. Roy works at Happy's Restaurant. He works 30 hours a week. Last week he earned $450, of which $150 was tips. How much is he paid per hour?

_____

SCIENCE CONNECTION

Use the following information for Exercise 23. The formula $m = d \times v$, where m = mass, d = density, and v = volume, can be solved as an equation if the values for two of the variables are known.

23. Gold has a density of 19.28 gm/cm^3. Use the formula to find the volume, in cubic centimeters, of a cube of gold with a mass of 2.41 grams.

_____

Division Equations

Write the operation you would use to solve each equation.

1. $\dfrac{n}{7} = 20$

2. $4p = 6.4$

3. $x + 1.5 = 3.5$

4. $81 = y - 12$

_____ _____ _____ _____

Solve each equation. Check your solutions.

5. $\dfrac{w}{3} = 8$

6. $\dfrac{n}{7} = 9$

7. $\dfrac{x}{10} = 17$

8. $\dfrac{b}{9} = 24$

_____ _____ _____ _____

9. $\dfrac{y}{0.8} = 2.9$

10. $4.2 = \dfrac{k}{6}$

11. $\dfrac{d}{4} = 37$

12. $4 = \dfrac{c}{17}$

_____ _____ _____ _____

13. $\dfrac{n}{0.47} = 22$

14. $43 = \dfrac{a}{4}$

15. $\dfrac{y}{1.4} = 35$

16. $24 = \dfrac{h}{31}$

_____ _____ _____ _____

MIXED APPLICATIONS

Write an equation for Exercises 17–18 and solve.

17. When the total cost of a rental boat was divided equally among 5 people, each person paid $15.50. Find the total cost of the rental boat.

_____

18. It cost $120 to charter a large fishing boat. Each person paid $30 toward the cost. How many people chartered the fishing boat?

_____

MIXED REVIEW

Solve each equation. Check your solutions.

19. $x + 12 = 25$

20. $\dfrac{y}{4} = 18$

21. $b - 3.2 = 1.5$

22. $6x = 48$

_____ _____ _____ _____

23. $\dfrac{k}{1.2} = 6$

24. $2.2p = 121$

25. $l + 29 = 73$

26. $m - 91 = 4$

_____ _____ _____ _____

Solving 1-Step Equations

Solve each equation. Check your solutions.

1. $a + 4 = -2$

2. $b - 2.5 = 2.5$

3. $0.25c = 4$

4. $d - 9.1 = 5.2$

5. $2.1e = 4.2$

6. $f + 3.4 = -2.1$

7. $g + 0.1 = 1$

8. $-\frac{2}{3}h = 6$

9. $\frac{4}{7}j = 28$

10. $k - 1.2 = 3.1$

11. $m + 4 = 1.01$

12. $-\frac{n}{3} = 3$

Write an equation for each word sentence.

13. The sum of 1.3 and a number is 3.2.

14. A number decreased by 6.3 is -6.3.

MIXED APPLICATIONS

Write an equation. Then solve.

15. There were $\frac{4}{5}$ as many cars at the race the second year as the first. If there were 32 cars the second year, how many cars were there the first year?

16. It snowed 2.4 inches less this month than it did last month. If it snowed 10.3 inches this month, how much did it snow last month?

MIXED REVIEW

17. 12% of 300 is what number? _____

18. What percent of 2,700 is 405? _____

19. 48 is 60% of what number? _____

20. What is 18% of 240? _____

21. What is 9% of 32? _____

22. What percent of 85 is 34? _____

Exploring 2-Step Equations

Name the two operations you would use to solve each equation in the order you would use them.

1. $\frac{n}{3} + 6 = 9$

2. $4x - 5 = 20$

3. $\frac{a}{2.5} - 1 = 4$

4. $85 = 8y + 21$

_____   _____   _____   _____

Solve each equation. Check your solutions.

5. $\frac{x}{5} + 4 = 9$

6. $\frac{d}{9} - 6 = 12$

7. $9w + 3 = 39$

8. $5c - 3 = 12$

_____   _____   _____   _____

9. $8b + 2 = 34$

10. $19 = 4a + 7$

11. $16 = \frac{t}{3} + 8$

12. $7k + 4 = 25$

_____   _____   _____   _____

Write an equation for each word sentence.

13. Seven less than the product of 11 and a number, c, is 70.

_____

14. Four more than the quotient of a number, n, and 8 is 28.

_____

MIXED APPLICATIONS

Solve Exercises 15 and 16.

15. The length of a swimming pool is 10 ft shorter than twice the width. The length is 35 ft. What is the width?

_____

16. Show the calculator key sequence you can use to solve the equation $\frac{x}{2.4} - 0.625 = 0.0625$.

_____

MATH CONNECTION

17. You can combine like terms to find the measures of the angles in a triangle. The sum of the measures of the angles of a triangle is 180°. Write and solve an equation to find the measures of the angles in this triangle.

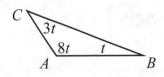

_____

Solving 2-Step Equations

Solve each equation. Check your solutions.

1. $2a + 5 = 1$

2. $4b - 1 = 7$

3. $0.5c - 12.25 = 2.25$

_____   _____   _____

4. $6t - 7 = -10$

5. $1.5h + 5 = 2$

6. $6y + 8 = 14$

_____   _____   _____

7. $-0.3j + 0.6 = 1.2$

8. $11k + 7.7 = 15.4$

9. $5w - {-2.5} = -7.5$

_____   _____   _____

10. $\frac{m}{3} + 8 = -7$

11. $\frac{3}{7}n - 7 = 5$

12. $\frac{7}{9}r + 3 = -4$

_____   _____   _____

Write the calculator key sequence you can use to solve each equation.

13. $3y = 4(6 - 5)$

14. $3(6 + 3) = 2z$

15. $7(2.1 - 3) = 3f$

_____   _____   _____

MIXED APPLICATIONS

Write an equation. Then solve.

16. Jason scored 3 fewer than twice as many goals this week as he did last week. He scored 15 goals this week. How many goals did he score last week?

_____

17. Ms. Phipps made 12 dolls for gifts this year. She made $4\frac{1}{2}$ times that number last year. Find the total number of dolls she made this year and last year.

_____

MIXED REVIEW

18. Which equation has a negative integer as its solution? Circle *a* or *b*.

   a. $2n - 6 = -12$ **b.** $14 - n = 6$

Equations with Fractions

Solve each equation. Check your solutions.

1. $n - \dfrac{1}{2} = \dfrac{41}{2}$

2. $q + \dfrac{1}{4} = \dfrac{53}{4}$

3. $6 = a + \dfrac{21}{3}$

4. $w - \dfrac{54}{5} = \dfrac{93}{10}$

_____

5. $\dfrac{3}{4}x = 6$

6. $\dfrac{6b}{5} = \dfrac{2}{3}$

7. $10 = \dfrac{21}{4}t$

8. $\dfrac{51}{6} = t + \dfrac{21}{3}$

_____

9. $\dfrac{z}{4} = \dfrac{103}{8}$

10. $9r = \dfrac{151}{2}$

11. $4h - \dfrac{21}{2} = 10$

12. $\dfrac{k}{3} - \dfrac{1}{2} = 12$

_____

MIXED APPLICATIONS

Solve Exercises 13 and 14.

13. Rod earned $60 in one week working for a lawn-care service. He worked for $6\frac{1}{4}$ hr. How much did he earn per hour?

14. Find the pattern in this sequence. Then write the next three terms in the sequence.
$5, 2\frac{1}{2}, 1\frac{1}{4}, \ldots$

MIXED REVIEW

Compare. Write $<$, $>$, or $=$.

15. 123 $\bigcirc$ 132

16. 2.14 $\bigcirc$ 2.140

17. $\dfrac{3}{4}$ $\bigcirc$ $\dfrac{2}{3}$

18. $6\frac{1}{8}$ $\bigcirc$ $6\frac{4}{32}$

Find each sum or difference.

19. $\dfrac{3}{4} + \dfrac{5}{6}$

20. $\dfrac{9}{10} - \dfrac{2}{3}$

21. $1\frac{4}{5} + 1\frac{1}{3}$

22. $6 - 3\frac{3}{5}$

Solving Equations

Solve each equation. Check your solutions.

1. $3x + 4 + 2x + 5 = 34$

_____

2. $2.5x - 5 + 3x + 8 = 19.5$

_____

3. $\frac{1}{2}x + 6 - 2x + \frac{1}{2} = \frac{7}{2}$

_____

4. $-10x - 3 - 2.5x + 20 = 67$

_____

5. $2(x + 1) + 4 = 12$

_____

6. $-3(x + 4) + 15 = -12$

_____

7. $15 - 3(x - 1) = 12$

_____

8. $3(x - 2) + 2(x + 1) = -14$

_____

9. $\frac{1}{2}(x + 8) - 15 = -3$

_____

10. $2.5(x + 2) + 4.5 + 1.5(x - 3) = 15$

_____

11. $3.2(x + 4) + 2^2 + 1.7(x - 3) = 27$

_____

12. $13 - (2x + 2) = 2(x + 2) + 3x$

_____

13. $5(2 - x) - 3(4 - 2x) = 20$

_____

14. $3(5 - x) - 2(5 + x) = 3(x + 1)$

_____

15. $2x(x + 3) = 2x^2 + 15$

_____

16. $6.4(x + 4) + 4^2 + 3.4(x - 3) = 54$

_____

17. $26 - 2(2x + 2) = 4(x + 2) + 6x$

_____

18. $30(50 - 10x) - 20(50 + 50x) = 30(10x + 1)$

_____

24

Equation Applications

Use the table below for Exercises 1–3.

	Club A	Club B	Club C
Monthly Membership Dues	$25	$55	$15
Private Lesson Fee	$30	$20	$40

1. After how many private lessons in one month is the total monthly cost of Club A equal to the total monthly cost at Club B?

   _____

2. After how many private lessons in one month is the total monthly cost of Club A equal to the total monthly cost at Club C?

   _____

3. After how many private lessons in one month is the total monthly cost of Club B equal to the total monthly cost at Club C?

   _____

4. Amanda's dad is twice as old as she is today. The sum of their ages is 66. Find the ages of Amanda and her dad.

   _____

5. When 142 is added to a number, the result is 64 more than 3 times the number. What is the number?

   _____

6. Juan buys a book on sale for 30% off its retail price. He pays $14.70 for the book. What is the retail price of the book?

   _____

7. 68 less than 5 times a number is equal to the number. What is the number?

   _____

Name _____   Date _____

Analyzing Solutions

For Exercises 1–3, use the properties of equality to simplify each equation. Tell whether the final equation is a true statement by writing *true* or *false*.

1. $4x - 3 = 2x + 13$ **2.** $4x - 5 = 2(2x - 1) - 3$ **3.** $4x + 2 = 4x - 5$

_____   _____   _____

When you simplify an equation using the properties of equality, you will find one of three results.

Result	What does this mean?	How many solutions?
$x = a$	When the value of x is a, the equation is a true statement.	1
$a = a$	Any value of x makes the equation a true statement.	Infinitely many
$a = b$	There is no value of x that makes the equation a true statement.	0

Use the following information and the table to solve Exercises 4 and 5. Tell whether each equation has one, zero, or infinitely many solutions.

4. $6 + 3x = x - 8$ **5.** $8x + 4 = 4(2x + 1)$

_____   _____

Complete each equation so that it has the indicated number of solutions.

6. No solutions: $3x + 1 = 3x +$ _____   **7.** Infinitely many: $2x - 4 = 2x -$ _____

Problem-Solving Strategy

WRITE AN EQUATION

Write an equation for each problem. Then solve.

1. Eric has saved $587.46 to buy a used car. The car he wants costs $675. How much more money does he need?

_____

2. A custom-made pair of shoes costs $225. This is 3 times the cost of a regular pair of shoes. What is the cost of a regular pair of shoes?

_____

3. A truck can carry 7 tons of logs. Suppose that a truck is carrying a load of 4.7 tons. How much more could it haul?

_____

4. A newspaper began publication in 1897 and was printed daily for 76 years. In what year did the newspaper stop publication?

_____

5. Vera used 2.4 gallons of paint to paint her living room. This is 4 times the amount she used for her kitchen. How much paint was used for the kitchen?

_____

6. The cost of a dinner is divided equally among 12 diners. Each diner pays $12.50 for his or her portion. What was the cost of the dinner?

_____

MIXED APPLICATIONS

7. Roy has a total of 10 quarters and dimes. The value of the coins is $2.05. He has more quarters than dimes. How many of each coin does he have?

_____

8. Dot wants to buy meat for $7.57, milk for $2.69, cereal for $4.08, and juice for $2.99. She has $16.00. Does she have enough money for all the items?

_____

9. Harvey bought a used car. He installed a $212 stereo system and 4 new tires valued at $285. His car is now worth $1,742. How much did he pay for the car?

_____

10. Marsha sold 2 cameras in January, 4 in February, 7 in March, and 11 in April. If the number sold increases at the same rate, how many cameras will she sell in December??

_____

Name _____ Date _____

Exploring Slides, Flips, and Turns

Draw a *flip*, *turn*, and *slide* for each figure. Show flip lines and direction arrows.

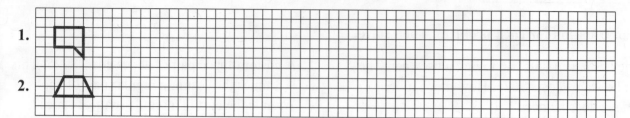

1.

2.

Tell how each polygon was moved. Write *flip*, *slide*, or *turn*.

3.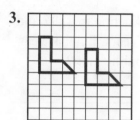

4.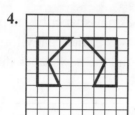

5.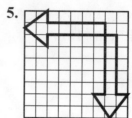

6.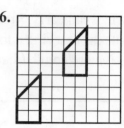

_____ _____ _____ _____

Solve.

7. Jo walks past the bakery on one side of Elm Street. How many turns must she make to be walking in the opposite direction on the other side of Elm Street?

_____

8. Miranda buys 5 boxes of 24 tiles to make a floor design. She uses all but 7 tiles. How many tiles does Miranda use for the floor design?

_____

EVERYDAY MATH CONNECTION

Use *flip*, *slide*, or *turn* to answer each question. Which motion do you use when you do each?

9. open a jar of peanut butter

_____

10. zip a jacket

_____

11. open a magazine

_____

12. screw in a light bulb

_____

Unit 3
Core Skills Math, Grade 8

Applying Transformations

Apply each transformation to the vertices of the original rectangle and give the coordinates of each vertex of the image.

	Vertices of Rectangle	(2, 2)	(2, 4)	(−3, 4)	(−3, 2)
1.	$(x, y) \rightarrow (x, {}^-y)$				
2.	$(x, y) \rightarrow (x + 2, y - 5)$				
3.	$(x, y) \rightarrow ({}^-x, y)$				
4.	$(x, y) \rightarrow ({}^-x, {}^-y)$				
5.	$(x, y) \rightarrow (x - 3, y + 1)$				

MIXED REVIEW

Use the table for Exercises 6–8.

Row-Along Canoe Rental Monthly Rental Income (in dollars)					
May	June	July	Aug.	Sept.	Oct.
$2,500	$5,050	$8,900	$8,750	$4,200	$1,800

6. mean _____

7. median _____

8. mode _____

Properties of Translations

1. Trace rectangle *ABCD* and triangle *PQR* on a piece of paper. Then cut out your traced figures.

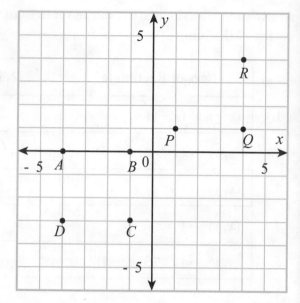

2. Place your copy of the rectangle on top of the rectangle in the figure. Then translate the rectangle by sliding your copy 6 units to the right and 1 unit down. Draw the new location of the rectangle on the coordinate plane and label the vertices *A'*, *B'*, *C'*, and *D'*.

3. Place your copy of the triangle on top of the triangle in the figure. Then translate the triangle by sliding your copy 5 units to the left and 2 units up. Draw the new location of the triangle on the coordinate plane and label the vertices *P'*, *Q'*, and *R'*.

4. Use a ruler to measure line segments $\overline{AD}$ and $\overline{PR}$. Then, measure $\overline{A'D'}$ and $\overline{P'R'}$. What do you notice?

_____

_____

5. Use a protractor to measure $\angle C$ and $\angle R$. Then, measure $\angle C'$ and $\angle R'$. What do you notice?

_____

_____

6. Count the pairs of parallel lines in rectangle *ABCD*. Count the pairs of parallel lines in rectangle *A'B'C'D'*. What do you notice?

_____

_____

WRITER'S CORNER

7. Use your results from Exercises 4–6 to write a conjecture about translations.

_____

_____

Properties of Reflections

1. Trace rectangle *ABCD* and triangle *PQR* on a piece of paper. Then, cut out your traced figures.

2. Place your copy of the rectangle on top of the rectangle in the figure. Then reflect the rectangle across the *x*-axis by flipping your copy across the *x*-axis. Draw the new location of the rectangle on the coordinate plane and label the vertices *A′*, *B′*, *C′*, and *D′*.

3. Place your copy of the triangle on top of the triangle in the figure. Then reflect the triangle across the *y*-axis by flipping your copy across the *y*-axis. Draw the new location of the triangle on the coordinate plane and label the vertices *P′*, *Q′*, and *R′*.

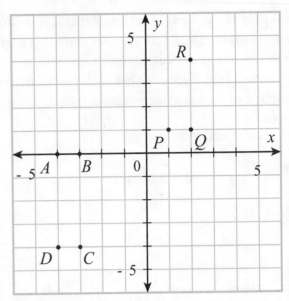

4. Use a ruler to measure line segments $\overline{BC}$ and $\overline{PR}$. Then, measure $\overline{B'C'}$ and $\overline{P'R'}$. What do you notice?

_____

_____

5. Use a protractor to measure ∠*D* and ∠*P*. Then, measure ∠*D′* and ∠*P′*. What do you notice?

_____

_____

6. Count the pairs of parallel lines in rectangle *ABCD*. Count the pairs of parallel lines in rectangle *A′B′C′D′*. What do you notice?

_____

_____

WRITER'S CORNER

7. Use your results from Exercises 4–6 to write a conjecture about reflections.

_____

_____

8. Using the triangle from Exercise 1, rotate your copy of the triangle 180° around the origin and draw the new location. Make measurements and observations to help you state a conjecture about rotations.

_____

_____

Combining Transformations

Apply the indicated series of transformations to the triangle. Each transformation is applied to the image of the previous translation, not the original figure. Label each image with the letter of the transformation applied.

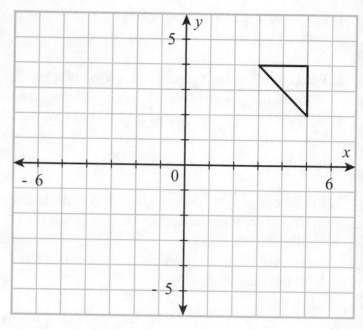

1. Reflection across the x-axis

2. $(x, y) \rightarrow (x - 3, y)$

3. Reflection across the y-axis

4. $(x, y) \rightarrow (x, y + 4)$

5. Rotation 90° clockwise around the origin

6. Compare the size and shape of the final image to that of the original figure.

_____

7. Write which combination of transformations changed figure *A* into figure *B*. Choose from *translation, rotation,* or *reflection*.

_____

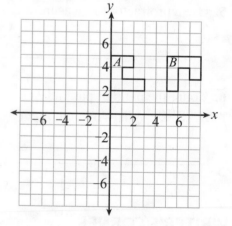

In the graph, *ABCD* is rotated and translated to form *A'B'C'D'*. Use <, >, or = to complete Exercises 8–10.

8. $AD \bigcirc A'D'$

9. $AD \bigcirc B'A'$

10. $\angle B \bigcirc \angle B'$

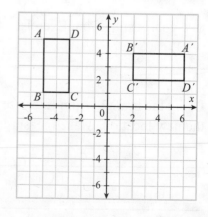

36

Congruent Figures

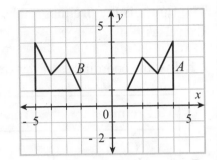

1. Identify a sequence of transformations that will transform figure A into figure B.

_____

2. Identify another sequence of transformations that transforms figure A into figure B.

_____

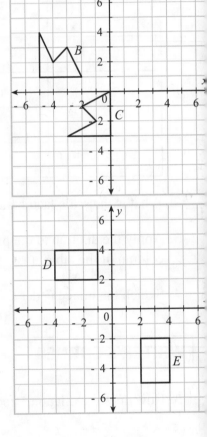

3. Any sequence of transformations that changes figure B into figure C will need to include a rotation. Identify a rotation around the origin that would result in the figure being oriented as figure C.

_____° counterclockwise

4. After the rotation you identified in Exercise 3, what transformation is necessary to result in figure C? _____

5. A sequence of transformations that changes figure D to figure E will need to include a rotation. Describe a rotation around the origin that would result in the figure being oriented as figure E.

_____° clockwise

6. After the rotation you identified in Exercise 5, what are the coordinates of the vertices of the rotated figure? _____

7. After the rotation you identified in Exercise 5, what transformation is necessary to result in figure E? _____

WRITER'S CORNER

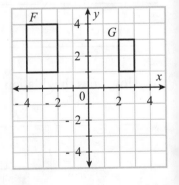

8. Is there a sequence of transformations that would transform figure F into figure G? Explain.

_____

_____

Enlargements

The figure is the preimage. The center of dilation is the origin. Use the graph and the table for Exercises 1–4.

1. List the coordinates of the vertices of the preimage in the first column of the table.

Preimage	Image
(2, 2)	(6, 6)

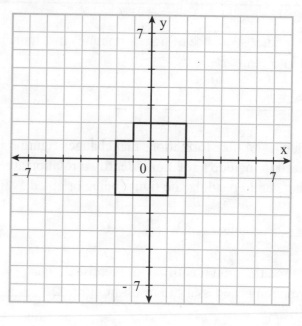

2. What is the scale factor for the dilation $(x, y) \rightarrow (3x, 3y)$? _____

3. Apply the dilation to the preimage and write the coordinates of the vertices of the image in the second column of the table.

4. Sketch the image under the dilation on the coordinate grid.

WRITER'S CORNER

5. How does the dilation affect the length of line segments?

_____

_____

6. How does the dilation affect angle measures?

_____

_____

Reductions

The arrow is the preimage. The center of dilation is the origin.

1. List the coordinates of the vertices of the preimage in the first column of the table.

Preimage	Image

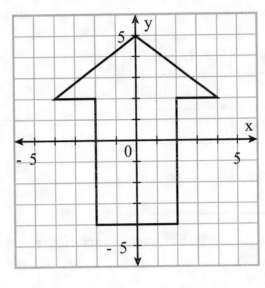

2. What is the scale factor for the dilation $(x, y) \rightarrow (\frac{1}{2}x, \frac{1}{2}y)$? _____

3. Apply the dilation to the preimage and write the coordinates of the vertices of the image in the second column of the table.

4. Sketch the image under the dilation on the coordinate grid.

WRITER'S CORNER

5. How does the dilation affect the length of line segments?

_____

_____

6. How would a dilation with scale factor 1 affect the preimage?

_____

_____

Dilations

1. The square is the preimage. The center of dilation is the origin. Write the coordinates of the vertices of the preimage in the first column of the table. Then apply the dilation $(x, y) \rightarrow (\frac{3}{2}x, \frac{3}{2}y)$ and write the coordinates of the vertices of the image in the second column. Sketch the image of the figure under the dilation.

Preimage	Image
(2, 0)	(3, 0)

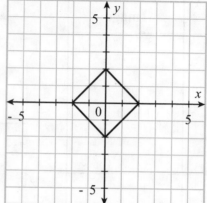

In Exercises 2 and 3, sketch the image of each figure under the given dilation.

2. $(x, y) \rightarrow (2x, 2y)$

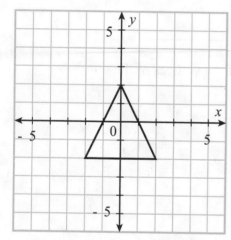

3. $(x, y) \rightarrow (\frac{2}{3}x, \frac{2}{3}y)$

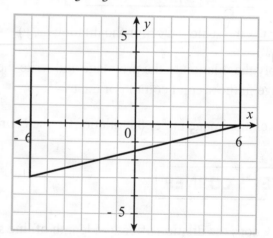

In Exercises 4 and 5, identify the scale factor of each dilation shown.

4. scale factor = _____

5. scale factor = _____

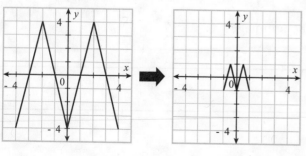

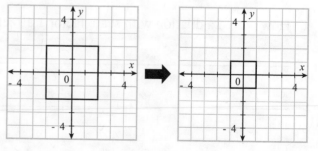

Transformations with Dilations

Apply the indicated series of transformations to the
rectangle. Each transformation is applied to the
image of the previous transformation, not to the
original figure. Label each image with the exercise
number of the transformation applied.

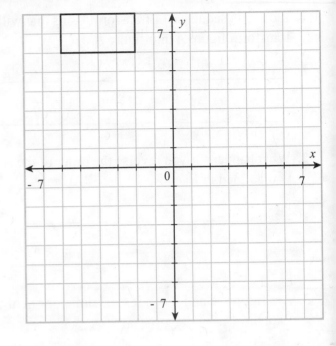

1. $(x, y) \rightarrow (x + 7, y - 2)$

2. $(x, y) \rightarrow (x, {}^{-}y)$

3. rotation 90° clockwise around the origin

4. $(x, y) \rightarrow (x + 5, y + 3)$

5. $(x, y) \rightarrow (3x, 3y)$

6. List the coordinates of the vertices of the rectangle formed in Exercise 5.

_____

7. Compare the following attributes of the rectangle formed in Exercise 5 to those of the original figure.

Shape	
Size	
Angle Measures	

Similar Figures

1. Identify a sequence of transformations that will transform figure *A* into figure *B*.

   _____

   _____

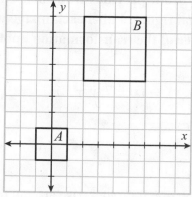

2. What happens if you reverse the order of the sequence you defined in Exercise 1?

   _____

   _____

3. Are figures *A* and *B* congruent, simlar, or neither? Explain.

   _____

   _____

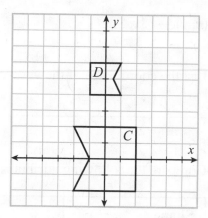

4. Identify a sequence of transformations that will transform figure *C* into figure *D*. Include a reflection.

   _____

   _____

5. Identify a sequence of transformations that will transform figure *C* into figure *D*. Include a rotation.

   _____

   _____

6. Circle the figures that are similar to each other.

   _____

   _____

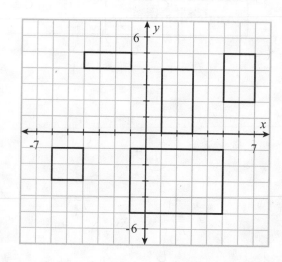

42

Estimating Sums and Differences

Choose the best estimate for each exercise. Circle *a*, *b*, or *c*.

1. $\frac{5}{6} + \frac{6}{7}$ **a.** 2   **b.** 1   **c.** $\frac{1}{2}$

2. $\frac{11}{12} - \frac{4}{9}$ **a.** 2   **b.** 1   **c.** $\frac{1}{2}$

3. $4\frac{1}{10} + 5\frac{1}{8}$ **a.** 8   **b.** 9   **c.** 10

Estimate each sum or difference.

4. $\frac{9}{20} + \frac{8}{15}$ 5. $\frac{9}{10} - \frac{4}{7}$ 6. $12\frac{1}{5} + 7\frac{7}{10}$ 7. $8\frac{2}{3} - 1\frac{1}{6}$

_____   _____   _____   _____

MIXED APPLICATIONS

8. One piece of jewelry contains $2\frac{1}{4}$ oz turquoise. Another contains $2\frac{13}{16}$ oz turquoise. About how much turquoise is in the two pieces of jewelry?

_____

9. Al got a difference of $\frac{13}{5}$ when he subtracted $\frac{2}{5}$ from $\frac{15}{10}$. Was his answer reasonable? Explain.

_____

EVERYDAY MATH CONNECTION

The price of a share of stock in a company is listed on a stock exchange as a fraction or a mixed number. This number represents dollars or parts of a dollar. A "+" sign means the stock value has risen by that much from its value on the previous day. A "-" sign means its value has fallen by that much.

10. Estimate the total change in price of Jarvis Microchip Corporation stock over a five-day period.

	Monday	Tuesday	Wednesday	Thursday	Friday
Jarvis Microchip	$36\frac{1}{2}$	$+\frac{1}{4}$	$+\frac{5}{8}$	$-\frac{1}{8}$	$+1\frac{7}{8}$

Estimate:

_____

_____

Adding and Subtracting

Find each sum or difference.

1. $\frac{2}{3} + -\frac{1}{3}$ _____

2. $-\frac{3}{8} + \frac{4}{8}$ _____

3. $-\frac{2}{9} + 3$ _____

4. $-\frac{2}{5} + -\frac{1}{5}$ _____

5. $\frac{2}{4} + -\frac{3}{4}$ _____

6. $-6 + -\frac{4}{7}$ _____

7. $-2.1 + -4.1$ _____

8. $0.3 + -0.9$ _____

9. $-4.21 + -7.12$ _____

10. $\frac{3}{4} - \frac{1}{3}$ _____

11. $-\frac{6}{7} - -\frac{1}{2}$ _____

12. $\frac{3}{13} - -\frac{7}{8}$ _____

13. $-\frac{4}{10} - -\frac{3}{5}$ _____

14. $-\frac{4}{11} - -\frac{13}{22}$ _____

15. $-\frac{5}{9} - -\frac{3}{18}$ _____

16. $-3.2 - -7.4$ _____

17. $0.12 - -8.63$ _____

18. $-7.21 - -12.4$ _____

19. $-2.11 - -6.9$ _____

20. $-13.2 - -6.41$ _____

21. $-21.6 - 9.09$ _____

MIXED APPLICATIONS

22. Marta is keeping track of how many dozen eggs she sells in a week. On Monday, she had 3 dozen eggs to sell. By Wednesday, she had gathered $2\frac{1}{2}$ dozen more from her hens. If by Friday she had only 3 eggs left, how many had she sold during the week?

_____

23. Rainie kept track of the temperature during January. Her figures showed the average temperatures for four weeks were 11.3°C, -4.7°C, -7.01°C, and -21.6°C. What was the difference between the highest and lowest weekly average temperature?

_____

NUMBER SENSE

24. If you add -5 to an integer and then subtract -3 from that sum, is the result less than or greater than the original number?

_____

Name _____ Date _____

Estimating Products

Estimate each product.

1. $\dfrac{3}{8} \times \dfrac{9}{10}$ _____

2. $\dfrac{4}{5} \times \dfrac{7}{9}$ _____

3. $1\dfrac{3}{7} \times 3\dfrac{7}{8}$ _____

4. $4\dfrac{1}{3} \times 3\dfrac{1}{10}$ _____

5. $5\dfrac{3}{5} \times 6\dfrac{3}{5}$ _____

6. $\dfrac{11}{12} \times 20$ _____

7. $3\dfrac{3}{4} \times 8$ _____

8. $\dfrac{7}{8} \times 10\dfrac{1}{7}$ _____

9. $3\dfrac{1}{6} \times 4 \times 5\dfrac{3}{4}$ _____

10. $1 \times 8 \times \dfrac{9}{16}$ _____

11. $12 \times \dfrac{11}{12} \times \dfrac{2}{5}$ _____

Estimate each product. Tell whether the estimate is an *overestimate*, an *underestimate*, or a *close estimate*.

12. $8\dfrac{1}{7} \times 7\dfrac{5}{6}$

_____

13. $5\dfrac{2}{9} \times 6\dfrac{1}{12}$

_____

14. $\dfrac{7}{8} \times \dfrac{3}{4}$

_____

15. $\dfrac{3}{8} \times 20\dfrac{1}{4}$

_____

16. $4\dfrac{4}{5} \times 9\dfrac{9}{10}$

_____

17. $7\dfrac{7}{12} \times 8\dfrac{1}{3}$

_____

MIXED APPLICATIONS

18. A farmer planted crops in a $119\dfrac{7}{8}$-acre field. Corn covered $\dfrac{3}{8}$ of the field. About how many acres of corn did the farmer plant?

_____

19. Matt bought a used lawn mower for $\dfrac{2}{5}$ of the $280 regular price. After using the mower for one year, he sold it for $\dfrac{7}{15}$ of what he had paid for it. For about how much did he sell the mower?

_____

EVERYDAY MATH CONNECTION

Here is a recipe for whole wheat crackers:

20. Estimate the amount of each ingredient needed to make $\dfrac{1}{2}$ the recipe.

Whole Wheat Crackers
$1\dfrac{7}{8}$ cups of whole wheat flour
$2\dfrac{1}{4}$ teaspoons salt
$\dfrac{3}{8}$ cup oil
$\dfrac{11}{12}$ tablespoon yeast

_____

_____

45

Estimating Quotients

Tell whether each quotient is *less than 1* or *greater than 1*.

1. $\frac{2}{3} \div \frac{1}{2}$ 2. $\frac{1}{4} \div \frac{2}{5}$ 3. $\frac{2}{5} \div \frac{4}{7}$ 4. $\frac{5}{6} \div \frac{1}{4}$

_____   _____   _____   _____

5. $\frac{1}{3} \div \frac{1}{2}$ 6. $\frac{5}{8} \div \frac{3}{5}$ 7. $\frac{11}{12} \div \frac{5}{6}$ 8. $\frac{2}{3} \div \frac{3}{4}$

_____   _____   _____   _____

9. $\frac{1}{6} \div \frac{1}{5}$ 10. $\frac{2}{9} \div \frac{1}{5}$ 11. $\frac{15}{16} \div \frac{1}{10}$ 12. $\frac{1}{2} \div \frac{6}{11}$

_____   _____   _____   _____

Use compatible numbers to estimate each quotient.

13. $9\frac{1}{4} \div 2\frac{7}{8}$ 14. $13\frac{5}{6} \div 7\frac{1}{3}$ 15. $4\frac{4}{5} \div 9\frac{9}{10}$

_____   _____   _____

16. $6\frac{1}{3} \div 6\frac{1}{4}$ 17. $8\frac{3}{8} \div \frac{5}{4}$ 18. $1\frac{3}{4} \div 3\frac{1}{9}$

_____   _____   _____

19. $15\frac{11}{14} \div 3\frac{8}{9}$ 20. $5\frac{1}{5} \div 15\frac{3}{8}$ 21. $5\frac{7}{10} \div 30\frac{2}{9}$

_____   _____   _____

MIXED APPLICATIONS

22. Julio fertilized 41 plants in $2\frac{1}{4}$ hours. About how many plants did Julio fertilize in 1 hour?

_____

23. Molly loads $64\frac{1}{3}$ lb of potatoes into $7\frac{3}{4}$ bags. About how many pounds of potatoes are in each bag?

_____

LOGICAL REASONING

24. Tim had some $1 bills in his wallet on Monday. He spent half of the bills on Tuesday, half of what was left on Wednesday, and half of what was left on Thursday. What fraction of the original number of $1 bills did he spend on Thursday?

_____

Multiplying and Dividing

Find each product or quotient. Write fractions in simplest form.

1. $\frac{2}{4} \cdot -\frac{1}{9}$ _____

2. $\frac{1}{5} \cdot \frac{3}{5}$ _____

3. $\frac{2}{7} \cdot -\frac{2}{3}$ _____

4. $-\frac{6}{9} \cdot \frac{8}{13}$ _____

5. $\frac{3}{6} \div -\frac{1}{2}$ _____

6. $-\frac{3}{9} \div \frac{2}{3}$ _____

7. $-\frac{1}{4} \div -\frac{4}{5}$ _____

8. $\frac{5}{12} \div -\frac{6}{7}$ _____

9. $-2.7 \cdot 0.4$ _____

10. $-11.4 \cdot 1.2$ _____

11. $-5 \cdot -0.2$ _____

12. $4.2 \div 0.21$ _____

13. $-5.2 \div 1.3$ _____

14. $5.13 \div -0.3$ _____

15. $-0.3 \cdot -0.4 \times -5.2$ _____

16. $\frac{1}{2} \cdot \left(16 \times -\frac{1}{15}\right)$ _____

Evaluate each expression for $l = -0.5$ and $w = \frac{3}{5}$.

17. $-15 \div w$ _____

18. $l \div 0.5$ _____

19. $w \cdot -2.8$ _____

20. $15.5 \cdot w$ _____

21. $-12.4 \cdot l$ _____

22. $w \div 0.2$ _____

23. $l \cdot 6.3$ _____

24. $l \cdot w$ _____

Find the value for n that makes each statement true.

25. $32 \div n = 4$ _____

26. $4 \cdot n = 1.6$ _____

27. $34 \div n = 17$ _____

MIXED APPLICATIONS

28. The length of a stake that is dug into the ground deteriorates 0.12 inch every winter. If the stake is 15.5 inches long, how long will it be after 6 winters?

_____

29. The lake in Chris's backyard increases in volume by 1.12 liters every year. How long will it take for Chris's lake to increase by 30.24 liters?

_____

WRITER'S CORNER

30. Write a word problem similar to one of the Mixed Applications problems. Solve.

_____

_____

Decimals for Fractions

Write a decimal for each fraction or mixed number.

1. $\dfrac{3}{4}$ _____

2. $\dfrac{7}{10}$ _____

3. $\dfrac{7}{20}$ _____

4. $\dfrac{9}{32}$ _____

5. $\dfrac{7}{50}$ _____

6. $\dfrac{2}{5}$ _____

7. $\dfrac{5}{16}$ _____

8. $\dfrac{13}{50}$ _____

9. $\dfrac{5}{8}$ _____

10. $1\dfrac{3}{4}$ _____

11. $\dfrac{3}{25}$ _____

12. $\dfrac{17}{20}$ _____

13. $\dfrac{7}{16}$ _____

14. $\dfrac{3}{11}$ _____

15. $\dfrac{7}{18}$ _____

16. $2\dfrac{5}{9}$ _____

17. $\dfrac{3}{40}$ _____

18. $3\dfrac{1}{8}$ _____

19. $\dfrac{11}{30}$ _____

20. $\dfrac{2}{15}$ _____

Compare. Write $<$, $>$, or $=$.

21. $1.2 \bigcirc 1\dfrac{2}{5}$

22. $\dfrac{3}{4} \bigcirc 0.7$

23. $0.5 \bigcirc \dfrac{1}{2}$

24. $0.8 \bigcirc \dfrac{3}{5}$

25. $1\dfrac{2}{3} \bigcirc 1.6$

26. $4\dfrac{1}{2} \bigcirc 4.50$

27. $0.25 \bigcirc \dfrac{1}{25}$

28. $8.6 \bigcirc 8\dfrac{5}{6}$

MIXED APPLICATIONS

29. Ed typed $4\dfrac{7}{8}$ pages of an office report. Write as a decimal the number of pages Ed typed.

_____

30. Kamaria completed a freestyle event in $2\dfrac{3}{5}$ min and a butterfly event in $2\dfrac{2}{3}$ min. Write as a decimal each event time. Which event was completed in the least time?

_____

MATH CONNECTION

31. Study your completed Exercises 1–30. Write a rule for predicting which fractions will have terminating decimals (HINT: Factor the denominators.)

_____

_____

48

Name _____ Date _____

Fractions for Decimals

Write a fraction in simplest form or a mixed number for each decimal.

1. 0.8 _____   **2.** 0.12 _____   **3.** 0.7 _____   **4.** 0.05 _____

5. 0.075 _____   **6.** 0.45 _____   **7.** 0.25 _____   **8.** 0.020 _____

9. 4.5 _____   **10.** 3.94 _____   **11.** 5.24 _____   **12.** 8.36 _____

13. 0.1 _____   **14.** 0.55 _____   **15.** 0.13 _____   **16.** 1.10 _____

17. 3.4 _____   **18.** 0.82 _____   **19.** 0.27 _____   **20.** 1.8 _____

Write in order from least to greatest.

21. $\frac{1}{3}, 0.3, \frac{2}{5}$

22. $0.\overline{8}, \frac{5}{6}, \frac{7}{8}, \frac{3}{4}$

23. $\frac{1}{2}, 0.4, \frac{6}{11}, 0.\overline{5}$

24. $0.38, \frac{1}{4}, \frac{1}{3}, 0.45$

25. $1.\overline{2}, 1.2, 1\frac{2}{7}, 1\frac{1}{4}$

26. $0.125, \frac{3}{25}, \frac{2}{9}, 0.\overline{1}$

MIXED APPLICATIONS

27. A bag of sunflower seeds weighs 0.35 lb. Write the weight as a fraction.

28. Anica said she picked up 10.3125 lb of aluminum cans. Bertha said that she picked up $10\frac{1}{3}$ lb of cans. Who picked up more aluminum cans?

MATH CONNECTION

A decimal in which a pattern may occur but no group of decimals repeats is call a nonterminating, nonrepeating decimal.

29. Write a decimal that does not terminate or repeat.

49

© Houghton Mifflin Harcourt Publishing Company

Unit 4
Core Skills Math, Grade 8

Problem Solving

CHOOSE A STRATEGY

1. A submarine's position in the ocean was -14 m. In 4 minutes, the submarine changed its position to -66 m. What was the average change in position per minute?

_____

2. Paul purchased a CD player and 5 CDs. The total he spent was $257.50, and the CD player cost $210. What was the average cost of each CD?

_____

3. The high temperature in October was 77°F. What was the low temperature in December if it was 84.7°F less than the high in October?

_____

4. The temperature at 10:00 in the morning was 45.7°F. The temperature at 4:00 in the afternoon was 87.7°F. What was the average hourly temperature increase during the 6 hours?

_____

5. The Chungs went on vacation and used a total of 435 gal of gas. They used 30 gal more than 2 times as much gas to get to their destination as to get home. How much gas did they use to get home?

_____

6. At the local computer store, there was a sale on computer disks. Brand A was on sale at $15 for a box of 10. Brand B was on sale at $19.60 for a box of 15. Which brand costs less per disk?

_____

SCIENCE CONNECTION

7. Write a problem about an airplane changing altitude over a 1-minute period. Solve.

_____

_____

Lines and Line Segments

Use the dots for Exercises 1 and 2.

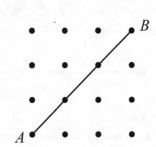

1. Draw two congruent line segments that are both parallel to $\overline{AB}$ and two-thirds as long as $\overline{AB}$.

2. Draw a line segment that is both congruent to $\overline{AB}$ and perpendicular to $\overline{AB}$.

Identify the two line segments as *parallel*, *perpendicular*, or *neither*. Also tell whether the line segments are congruent.

3.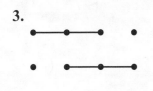

4.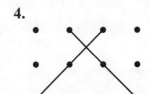

5.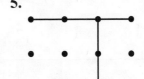

6.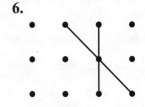

_____ _____   _____ _____

7. Bisect $\overline{HQ}$.

8. Construct a line perpendicular to $\overleftrightarrow{CD}$ at point E.

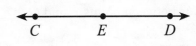

_____   _____

MIXED APPLICATIONS

Complete the statements in Exercises 9 and 10.

9. If $\overleftrightarrow{RS}$ bisects $\overline{XY}$ at P, then $\overline{XP} \cong$ _____

10. If $\overleftrightarrow{AB}$ is perpendicular to $\overleftrightarrow{CD}$ and $\overleftrightarrow{CD}$ is perpendicular to $\overleftrightarrow{EF}$, then $\overleftrightarrow{AB}$ is _____ to $\overleftrightarrow{EF}$.

LOGICAL REASONING

11. How many bisectors would you need to construct if you start with a 12-inch line segment and want to construct a $\frac{3}{8}$-inch line segment?

_____

Basic Ideas in Geometry

Using the letters *a, b, c, d, e, f, g,* or *h,* match one or more names from the list below with each figure in Exercises 1–4.

1. _____   **2.** 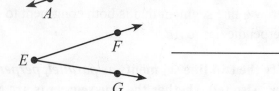 _____

3.  _____   **4.** 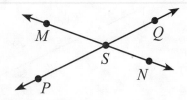 _____

a. $\overrightarrow{AB}$ **b.** $\angle FEG$ **c.** $\overline{RS}$ **d.** $\overleftarrow{BA}$ **e.** $\overrightarrow{TV}$ **f.** $\angle GEF$ **g.** $\angle E$ **h.** $\overrightarrow{TU}$

Use this line for Exercises 5 and 6.

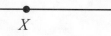

5. Name the line in three different ways.   **6.** Name three line segments.

_____   _____

Write *true* or *false* for each statement. Use lines *MN* and *PQ*, which intersect at *S.*

7. Point *S* is between points *P* and *Q.* _____

8. Point *S* is on $\overleftrightarrow{MN}$. _____

9. Point *S* is on $\overrightarrow{PQ}$. _____

10. Another name for $\overleftrightarrow{MS}$ is $\overleftrightarrow{SM}$. _____

MIXED APPLICATIONS

11. Segment *CD* contains point *A.* Draw *CD.* Can the segment be renamed as *CA*? Why or why not?

_____

12. Draw angle *JKL.* Name the angle in three different ways.

_____

LOGICAL REASONING

13. What is the minimum number of points needed to identify a line? a plane?

_____

Justifying Angle Relationships

Use the figure for Exercises 1–4.

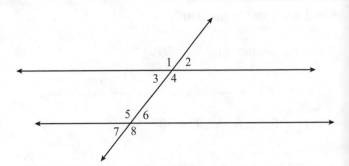

1. Name a pair of corresponding angles.

_____

2. Name a pair of alternate exterior angles.

_____

3. Name the relationship between ∠3 and ∠6. _____

4. Name the relationship between ∠4 and ∠6. _____

For parallel lines intersected by a transversal, tell whether each type of angle pair is *congruent* or *supplementary*.

5. alternate interior angles _____

6. linear pair _____

7. corresponding angles _____

8. same-side interior angles _____

9. vertical angles _____

10. alternate exterior angles _____

Use the following figure for Exercises 11–14. Write *true* or *false* to complete each exercise.

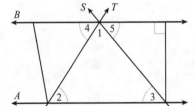

11. ∠1 + ∠2 + ∠5 are supplementary. _____

12. ∠2 + ∠4 + ∠5 are complementary. _____

13. ∠2 + ∠3 − ∠5 are complementary. _____

14. ∠4 + ∠5 + ∠1 = ∠2 + ∠3 + ∠1. _____

MIXED REVIEW

Find each sum or difference.

15. $5\frac{2}{3} + 3\frac{1}{2}$

16. $3.429 - 8.627$

_____

_____

17. $7.866 + 9.3 + 4.057 + 0.55$

18. $13\frac{5}{8} - 11\frac{1}{16}$

_____

_____

53

Name _____ Date _____

Finding Unknown Angle Measures

Find each angle measure.

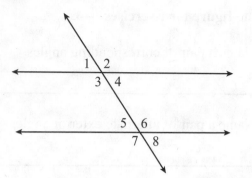

1. m ∠2 when m ∠1 = 30°

_____

2. m ∠6 when m ∠1 = 30°

_____

3. m ∠7 when m ∠3 = 150°

_____

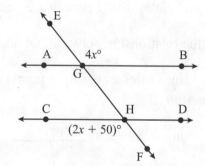

4. m∠EGB _____

5. m∠AGH _____

6. m∠DHF _____

Use the following figure for exercises 7–12. Write *true* or *false* to complete the exercise.

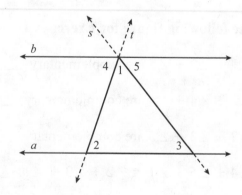

7. ∠1 = 180° − (∠4 + ∠5) _____

8. ∠1 = 90° − ∠3 _____

9. ∠1 = 180° − (∠2 + ∠3) _____

10. ∠1 = 90° − (∠2 − ∠3) _____

11. ∠1 = 180° − ∠3 + ∠4 _____

12. ∠1 = 180° − ∠3 − ∠4 _____

MIXED REVIEW

Find each product or quotient.

13. 3.287×5.1

_____

14. $\dfrac{3}{5} \div 2\dfrac{3}{10}$

_____

15. $78.592 \div 0.523$

_____

16. $\dfrac{9}{10} \times 8\dfrac{9}{10}$

_____

© Houghton Mifflin Harcourt Publishing Company

Unit 5
Core Skills Math, Grade 8

Name _____ Date _____

Exploring Parallel Lines and Transversals

Use the figure to find the measure of each given angle.

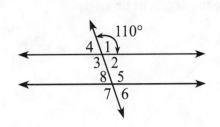

1. m∠2 = _____   **2.** m∠3 = _____

3 m∠4 = _____   **4.** m∠5 = _____

5. m∠6 = _____   **6.** m∠8 = _____

Tell whether the lines appear to be *parallel* or *perpendicular*.

7.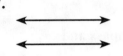

8.

9.

10.

_____   _____   _____   _____

Use the figure at the right for Exercises 11–19. Name the corresponding angles.

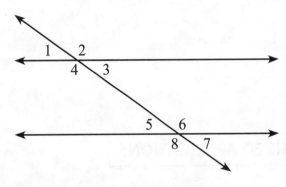

11. ∠1 and _____   **12.** ∠2 and _____

13. ∠3 and _____   **14.** ∠4 and _____

15. Name four pairs of vertical angles.

_____

Name the alternate interior angles in Exercises 16 and 17.

16. ∠4 and _____   **17.** ∠3 and _____

Name the alternate exterior angles in Exercises 18 and 19.

18. ∠1 and _____   **19.** ∠2 and _____

LOGICAL REASONING

Tell whether the labeled lines are parallel.

20. _____

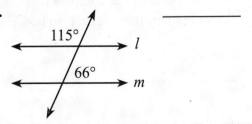

21. _____

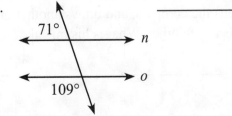

Exploring Bisecting Segments and Angles

Bisect each segment or angle.

1.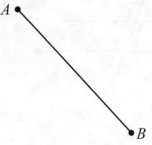

2.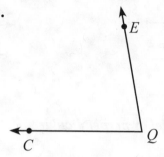

3.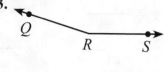

Draw the figures using a ruler and a protractor. Construct bisectors using a compass and straightedge.

4. a 5-cm line segment

5. a 96° angle

MIXED APPLICATIONS

6. A painting is 36 in. wide. Mark wants the painting to be centered on a wall that is 144 in. wide. How much wall space will be left on each side of the painting?

7. Ray *EF* bisects ∠*DEG*. m∠*DEF* = 43°. What is m∠*DEG*?

LOGICAL REASONING

8. Stu uses a compass and a straightedge to bisect $\overline{AB}$. He places the point of the compass on point *A*, opens the compass, and draws an arc that intersects $\overline{AB}$. He places the point of the compass on point *B*, opens the compass, and draws another arc that intersects $\overline{AB}$. Stu realizes that the arcs do not intersect each other. What is his mistake?

Constructing Congruent Triangles

Use the indicated rule to construct a triangle congruent to the given triangle.

1. SSS

2. SAS

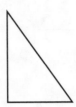

3. ASA

Each pair of triangles in Exercises 4 and 5 is congruent. Find the missing measures.

4.

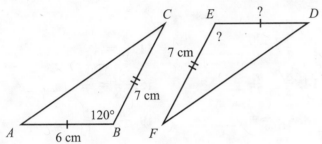

5.

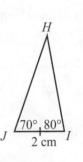

_____   _____

MIXED APPLICATIONS

6. Two cabins are located at points *A* and *B* on either side of a lake. To find the distance *AB* between the cabins, Mika measures the distances *PA, PB, PC,* and *PD*. How will Mika use this information to find *AB*?

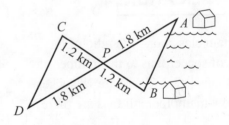

_____

_____

LOGICAL REASONING

7. In quadrilateral *PQRS*, $\overline{SQ}$ bisects ∠*PSR* to form triangle *PSQ* and triangle *RSQ*. $\overline{PS} \cong \overline{RS}$. Are the two triangles congruent? Why or why not?

_____

_____

Proportions

Write a proportion using two of the ratios.

1. $\frac{36}{46}, \frac{24}{32}, \frac{3}{4}$

2. $\frac{3}{8}, \frac{42}{104}, \frac{69}{184}$

3. 7 to 10, $\frac{280}{444}$, 70:111

_____   _____   _____

Write the equation that results when you cross multiply.

4. $\frac{1}{7} = \frac{30}{n}$

5. $\frac{6}{13} = \frac{n}{10}$

6. $\frac{n}{4} = \frac{8}{25}$

7. $\frac{200}{n} = \frac{100}{1}$

_____   _____   _____   _____

Solve each proportion.

8. $\frac{4}{5} = \frac{12}{n}$ _____

9. $\frac{1}{7} = \frac{n}{119}$ _____

10. $\frac{5}{1} = \frac{90}{n}$ _____

11. $\frac{4}{9} = \frac{n}{36}$ _____

12. $\frac{6}{7} = \frac{24}{n}$ _____

13. $\frac{7}{12} = \frac{n}{96}$ _____

14. $\frac{8}{3} = \frac{n}{27}$ _____

15. $\frac{5}{28} = \frac{45}{n}$ _____

16. $\frac{3}{3} = \frac{n}{200}$ _____

17. $\frac{5}{6} = \frac{n}{126}$ _____

18. $\frac{3}{10} = \frac{21}{n}$ _____

19. $\frac{n}{55} = \frac{5}{11}$ _____

20. $\frac{3}{8} = \frac{n}{0.48}$ _____

21. $\frac{1.8}{n} = \frac{12}{17}$ _____

22. $\frac{3}{7} = \frac{4.2}{n}$ _____

23. $\frac{4}{5} = \frac{n}{2.45}$ _____

MIXED APPLICATIONS

24. In a certain classroom, the ratio of the number of soccer fans to the number of football fans is 3:2. There are 18 soccer fans. How many football fans are there?

25. To paint the outside walls of their house, the Wagners mix blue paint and white paint in the ratio 2:3.5. How many gallons of white paint will they need to mix with 12 gal of blue paint?

_____   _____

EVERYDAY MATH CONNECTION

26. A racing bicycle has a gear ratio of 38 to 19. This means that the front chain ring has 38 teeth and the rear sprocket has 19 teeth. Another racing bicycle has a 44-tooth chain ring. How many teeth on the rear sprocket must the second racing bicycle have in order for the gear ratios of the two bicycles to be the same?

_____

Finding the Percent One Number Is of Another

Find each percent.

1. What percent of 36 is 12? _____
2. What percent of 56 is 42? _____

3. 48 is what percent of 60? _____
4. 9 is what percent of 60? _____

5. What percent of 42 is 14? _____
6. 90 is what percent of 120? _____

7. 26 is what percent of 39? _____
8. What percent of 72 is 18? _____

9. What percent of 80 is 20? _____
10. What percent of 76 is 95? _____

11. What percent of 120 is 15? _____
12. 12 is what percent of 40? _____

13. 30 is what percent of 80? _____
14. What percent of 15 is 7? _____

15. What percent of 72 is 36? _____
16. 96 is what percent of 48? _____

17. What percent of 75 is 15? _____
18. What percent of 110 is 44? _____

19. 32 is what percent of 10? _____
20. What percent of 700 is 175? _____

MIXED APPLICATIONS

21. Magic Smith made 70 free throws out of 105 attempts during the basketball season. What percent of the attempted free throws did he make?

22. In Luis's stamp collection, $\frac{3}{4}$ of the stamps are foreign. Of his foreign stamps, $\frac{1}{2}$ are French. What fraction of Luis's collection are the French stamps?

WRITER'S CORNER

23. Write a percent word problem that can be solved using the ratio $\frac{146}{365}$.

_____

_____

59

Estimating Percents

Name _____ Date _____

Choose the best estimate. Write *a*, *b*, or *c*.

1. 20% of 49 _____
   a. 20% of 40
   b. 20% of 30
   c. 20% of 50

2. 25% of $81.25 _____
   a. 25% of $80
   b. 25% of $90
   c. 25% of $70

3. 150% of $41.50 _____
   a. $40
   b. $60
   c. $80

Write the common ratio that is nearly equivalent to each percent.

4. 32% _____   5. 78% _____   6. 65% _____   7. 89% _____

Estimate each percent.

8. $\frac{42}{160}$ _____   9. 88:180 _____   10. 14 out of 18 _____

11. 82 of 123 is about what percent?

12. 147 is about what percent of 300?

Estimate each number.

13. 25% of what number is 69?

14. 50% of what number is 797?

MIXED APPLICATIONS

15. On a certain day, 112 of the 330 students brought their lunch to school. Estimate what percent of the students brought their lunch.

16. The number of flower seeds planted this year is a multiple of 8 and also a multiple of 7. The number of seeds planted is between 70 and 120. How many seeds were planted this year?

NUMBER SENSE

17. Using the signs + and −, complete the number sentence.

   10% of 240 ☐ 25% of 180 ☐ 110% of 50 is 14.

60

Name _____ Date _____

Problem-Solving Strategy

USE ESTIMATION

Estimate a 15% tip for each bill.

1. $18.35

2. $24.60

3. $5.74

4. $12.05

_____

_____

_____

_____

5. $31.99

6. $29.67

7. $21.04

8. $9.82

_____

_____

_____

_____

9. Gabriel and his four friends ate dinner at a restaurant. The total bill was $68. Gabriel wanted to leave a 15% tip. Estimate the amount of the tip.

10. The cost of a dinner for four was $46.00. This included the amount for a 15% tip. Estimate the amount of dinner alone.

MIXED APPLICATIONS

Solve.

11. Rose borrowed $8,000 for 6 yr at an interest rate of 8% per yr. How much did she pay in interest? What was the total amount she paid?

12. You enter a maze and walk 8 paces forward, turn right and walk 5 paces, turn right and walk 2 paces, turn left and walk 3 paces, turn left and walk 6 paces, turn left and walk 11 paces, turn left and walk 12 paces. How many paces are you from the entrance?

GEOGRAPHY CONNECTION

13. Lake Erie has an area of 9,910 square miles. The area of Great Bear Lake is about 20% greater than the area of Lake Erie. Estimate the area of Great Bear Lake.

Unit 6
Core Skills Math, Grade 8

Properties

Name the property shown in each exercise.

1. $5 + 8 = 8 + 5$ _____

2. $4 \times (7 + 2) = (4 \times 7) + (4 \times 2)$ _____

3. $(3 \times 2) \times 6 = 3 \times (2 \times 6)$ _____

4. $25 = 25 + 0$ _____

5. $7 \times 9 = 9 \times 7$ _____

6. $1 \times 36 = 36$ _____

7. $5 \times (3 - 2) = (5 \times 3) - (5 \times 2)$ _____

Complete.

8. $139 + \boxed{} = 139$

9. $212 \times \boxed{} = 212$

10. $35 + (17 + 25) = 35 + (\boxed{} + 17) = (35 + 25) + 17 = \boxed{} + 17 = \boxed{}$

MIXED APPLICATIONS

11. Amy bought 4 pens for $0.90 each and 4 folders for $0.15 each. Use the Distributive Property to determine how much she paid.

_____

12. Show how to rewrite $21 + 47 + 9$ using the Associative and Commutative Properties so you can use mental math to find the sum.

_____

MIXED REVIEW

Compare. Write $<$, $>$, or $=$.

13. $1.23 \bigcirc 12.3$

14. $3,704 \bigcirc 3,470$

Round to the nearest tenth.

15. 15.049 _____

16. 134.651 _____

Using Properties of Integers

Name the property shown.

1. -13 + 3 = 3 + -13

_____

2. -6 + 0 = -6

_____

3. $10 \cdot (-4 \cdot 3) = (10 \cdot -4) \cdot 3$

_____

4. $-7 \cdot 1 = -7$

_____

5. -2 + 2 = 0

_____

6. $15 \cdot (-6 + 4) = (15 \cdot -6) + (15 \cdot 4)$

_____

Use the properties to find each answer. Use mental math where possible.

7. (-3 + 5) + -6 = _____

8. $14 \times (10 + 7) =$ _____

9. -23 + 25 + 0 = _____

10. -13 + 20 + 13 + 13 = _____

11. -13 + 0 + 7 + -4 = _____

12. 422 − 40 + 40 = _____

13. 62 + 13 − 13 − 55 = _____

14. $(-8 \times 13) + (-8 \times 7) =$ _____

MIXED APPLICATIONS

15. A fashion designer bought 3 pieces of cloth each 6 m long, 4 pieces each 10 m long, and 2 pieces each 5 m long. What is the total number of meters of cloth?

_____

16. A writer wrote 30 lines on a page, deleted 15 lines, added 12 lines, and deleted 5 lines. How many lines were left on the page?

_____

PHYSICAL EDUCATION CONNECTION

17. Mike jogs every day. If he jogs 3 mi a day for 5 days of the week and then twice that distance on Saturdays and Sundays, what is the total distance he jogs in a week?

_____

Rational Numbers

Write each rational number in the form $\frac{a}{b}$.

1. 0.5 _____

2. $-2\frac{1}{3}$ _____

3. 4 _____

4. 2.6 _____

5. 0.8 _____

6. $-3\frac{3}{4}$ _____

7. 2.25 _____

8. $1\frac{4}{5}$ _____

Compare. Write <, >, or =.

9. $\frac{1}{7} \bigcirc -\frac{1}{7}$

10. $-0.8 \bigcirc 0.8$

11. $\frac{3}{4} \bigcirc \frac{4}{5}$

12. $-1.5 \bigcirc \frac{3}{5}$

Write in order from least to greatest.

13. $-2, \frac{1}{4}, -1\frac{2}{3}$

_____

14. $\frac{3}{4}, \frac{4}{7}, 1\frac{2}{3}, 2, 2.3$

_____

15. $-1.3, -1\frac{1}{3}, \frac{3}{6}, \frac{2}{5}, \frac{2}{3}$

_____

16. $1.45, 1\frac{2}{5}, 2.7, 2\frac{3}{8}, 1$

_____

MIXED APPLICATIONS

17. At 7:00 A.M., the temperature was $-12.3°$F. At 8:00 A.M., it was $-13.7°$F. At which time was it colder?

_____

18. A U.S. submarine is 220.8 ft below sea level. Then its position changes to 221.3 ft below sea level. Did it descend or rise?

_____

SCIENCE CONNECTION

Find each temperature in degrees Celsius.

To convert temperatures from degrees Fahrenheit to degrees Celsius, subtract 32° and multiply by $\frac{5}{9}$.

19. 50°F _____

20. 104°F _____

21. 0°F _____

Exploring Irrational Numbers

Complete the table. Then classify each number by placing an ✓ in each appropriate column. The first exercise has been done.

		Real Number	Rational Number	Whole Number	Integer	Irrational Number
1.	210	✓	✓	✓	✓	
2.	312					
3.	‑9.1					
4.	3.14159…					
5.	‑√13					
6.	‑10					
7.	$6\frac{1}{3}$					
8.	$(0.39)^2$					
9.	7.21212…					

10. Order the numbers in Exercises 1–9 from least to greatest.

_____

Find the positive square root. Then classify it as *a real, a rational, a whole, an irrational number,* or *an integer.*

11. 49 _____

12. 14 _____

13. 0.18 _____

14. 0.81 _____

SCIENCE CONNECTION

15. In electronics, power is equal to the square of the voltage divided by the resistance of a circuit. If the power is equal to 7, which of these resistances will yield a rational-number voltage: 7, 14, 63, 4, 28?

_____

Evaluating Expressions

Evaluate each expression.

1. $5 \cdot 2 + 1$

_____

2. $5(2 + 1)$

_____

3. $(4 + 6)(8)$

_____

4. $4 + 6 \cdot 8$

_____

5. $2(9 + 3)$

_____

6. $2 \cdot 9 + 3$

_____

7. $18 - (3 \cdot 6)$

_____

8. $(18 - 3)(6)$

_____

9. $8 \cdot 5 - 1$

_____

10. $8(5 - 1)$

_____

11. $2 \cdot 10 - 7$

_____

12. $2(10 - 7)$

_____

13. $\dfrac{4 + 8}{3}$

_____

14. $\dfrac{7 + 9}{4}$

_____

15. $\dfrac{11(2) + 18}{8}$

_____

16. $\dfrac{10 - 2(3)}{2}$

_____

17. $\dfrac{6 + 10}{2 + 2}$

_____

18. $\dfrac{10}{2} - \dfrac{6}{2}$

_____

19. $\dfrac{12}{16} + \dfrac{21}{4}$

_____

20. $\dfrac{12 + 21}{7 - 4}$

_____

21. $\dfrac{1}{2}(6 + 26)$

_____

22. $\dfrac{1}{2}(6) + \dfrac{1}{2}(26)$

_____

23. $\dfrac{2}{3}(18) - 9$

_____

24. $\dfrac{2}{3}(18 - 9)$

_____

Unit 7
Core Skills Math, Grade 8

Name _____ Date _____

Exploring Functions

Make a mapping diagram to represent the ordered pairs of each of the relations.

1.

x	y
3	9
2	4
1	1
0	0
-1	1
-2	4

2.

x	y
-8	-3
-8	3
-3	-2
-3	2
0	-1

3. In which diagram does each element of the domain match only one element of the range?

_____

_____

Is each relation a function? Write _yes_ or _no_. Explain.

4. {(1, 4), (2, 4), ((3, 5)}

_____

_____

_____

5. {(2, 3), (5, 3), (5, 5)}

_____

_____

_____

6.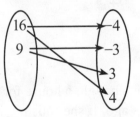

_____

_____

_____

7.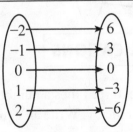

_____

_____

_____

VISUAL THINKING

8. Begin with a square with a side of 1 unit. Make a new square using the diagonal of the first square. Continue this pattern to form 4 squares. Find the area of the fourth square.

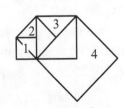

_____

67

© Houghton Mifflin Harcourt Publishing Company

Unit 8
Core Skills Math, Grade 8

Graphing Functions

Graph each set of ordered pairs. Tell whether each graph represents a function. Write *yes* or *no*.

1. {(-1, -4), (0, -1), (1, 2), (2, 5)}

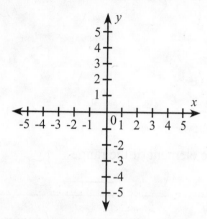

2. {(-1, -3), (0, -1), (1, 1), (1, 3)}

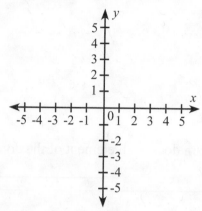

Graph the points that represent the relation. Tell whether the graph represents a function. Write *yes* or *no*.

3. Domain   Range _____

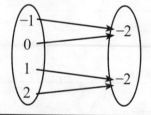

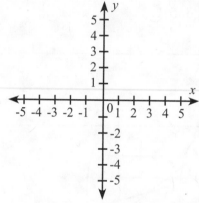

MIXED APPLICATIONS

4. Two less than three times a number, *x*, is equal to a number, *y*. Write an equation. Show three solutions for the equation. Tell whether the equation represents a function by writing *yes* or *no*.

_____

5. Mrs. Hans bought a house for $35,000 ten years ago. If she sells it this year for $119,000, what percent profit will she make?

_____

NUMBER SENSE

6. In the sequence 1, 2, 3, 4, 5, …, the value of any term in the sequence equals *n*, the number of the term itself. Write an expression, in terms of n, that will give the value of any term in the sequence 1, 4, 9, 16, 25.

_____

Name _____ Date _____

Relations and Functions

Write the ordered pairs for each relation. Write *yes* if the relation is a function and *no* if it is not.

1. 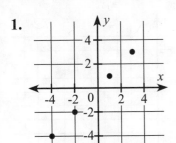   _____

     _____

2. 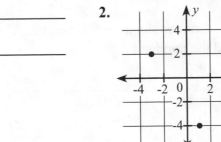   _____

     _____

Write a word rule for each relation in Exercises 3 and 4

3.

Wages of Employees				
Hours, x	10	20	25	30
Wages, y	$100	$200	$250	$300

4.

Sale Prices				
Original price, x	$15	$20	$22	$28
Sale price, y	$10	$15	$17	$23

_____   _____

MIXED APPLICATIONS

5. Kathy bought a new plant for her room. It will grow 4 in. every year. It is now 24 in. high. Make a table to show the relation between the height of the plant and the number of years for the next 5 years.

6. Michael spends 20% of his horseback riding time riding downhill. If he rode for 15 hr this week, how much time did he ride downhill?

_____

WRITER'S CORNER

7. The word rule for a relation is "divide the x-value by 2." Write a problem in which two items or situations show this relation.

_____

Problem-Solving Strategy

USE A GRAPH

1. Twice one number is equal to 1 more than a second number. The sum of the numbers is 5. Find the numbers.

_____

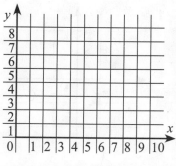

2. The difference between the length and width of a rectangle is 7 cm. The perimeter of the rectangle is 22 cm. Find the length and the width. (Remember, $P = 2l + 2w$).

_____

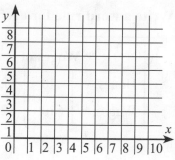

3. The perimeter of a rectangle is 18 inches. The length is twice the width. Find the length and the width.

_____

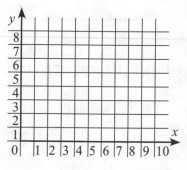

4. The sum of two numbers is 10. Five times the first number plus three times the second number is 36. Find the numbers.

_____

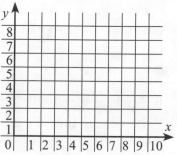

5. Matthew mixes pretzels that sell for $1.50 a pound with cereal that sells for $3.00 a pound. He wants to make 12 pounds of a mixture to sell for $2.00 a pound. How many pounds of each should he use?

_____

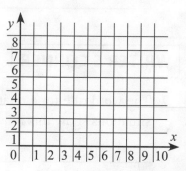

Name _____ Date _____

Interpreting Graphs

A roller coaster park is open from May to October each year. The graph shows the number of park visitors in one season.

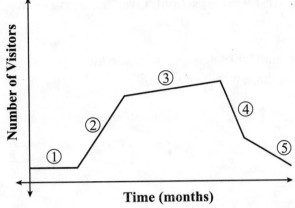

1. Segment 1 shows that attendance during the opening days of the park's season stayed constant. Describe what Segment 2 shows.

_____

_____

2. Based on the time frame, give a possible explanation for the change in attendance represented by Segment 2.

_____

_____

3. Which segments of the graph show decreasing attendance? Give a possible explanation.

_____

_____

WRITER'S CORNER

4. Explain how the slope of each segment of the graph is related to whether attendance increases or decreases.

_____

_____

_____

_____

Sketching a Graph for a Situation

Mrs. Sutton provides free math tutoring to her students every day after school. No one comes to tutoring sessions during the first week of school. Over the next two weeks, use of the tutoring service gradually increases.

1. Sketch a graph showing the number of students who use the tutoring service over the first three weeks of school.

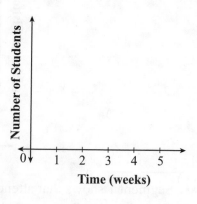

2. Mrs. Sutton's students are told that they will have a math test at the end of the fifth week of school. How do you think this will affect the number of students who come to tutoring?

_____

_____

3. Considering your answer to Exercise 2, sketch a graph showing the number of students who might use the tutoring service over the first six weeks of school.

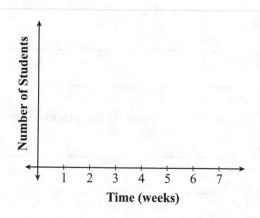

4. Suppose Mrs. Sutton offered bonus credit to students who came to tutoring sessions. How do you think this would affect the number of students who come to tutoring?

_____

_____

5. How would your answer to Exercise 4 affect the graph?

_____

_____

Name _____   Date _____

Analyzing Graphs

In a lab environment, colonies of bacteria follow a predictable pattern of growth. The graph shows this growth over time. Use the graph for Exercises 1–3.

1. During which phase is growth slowest? During which phase is growth fastest? Explain.

_____

_____

_____

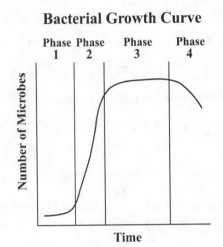

Bacterial Growth Curve

2. What is happening to the population during Phase 3?

_____

_____

_____

3. What is happening to the population during Phase 4?

_____

A woodland area on an island contains a population of foxes. The graph describes the changes in the fox population over time. Use the graph for Exercises 4–6.

4. What is happening to the fox population before time *t*?

_____

_____

5. At time *t*, a conservation organization moves a large group of foxes to the island. Sketch a graph to show how this action might affect the population on the island after time *t*.

6. At some point after time *t*, a forest fire destroys part of the woodland area on the island. Describe how your graph from Exercise 5 might change.

_____

_____

_____

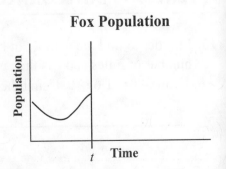

Fox Population

Equations with Two Variables

Write four ordered pairs that are solutions of each equation.

1. $y = x + 5$ **2.** $y = x - 3$ **3.** $y = 2x$

_____   _____   _____

_____   _____   _____

Determine whether each ordered pair is a solution of $y = 3x - 4$. Write *yes* or *no*.

4. $(5, 1)$ **5.** $(-2, 2)$ **6.** $(1, -1)$ **7.** $\left(\frac{1}{3}, 4\right)$

_____   _____   _____   _____

Rewrite each equation to express y in terms of x. Then find the y-values for each equation when $x = -1, -\frac{1}{2}, 0, \frac{1}{2}$, and 1.

8. $x + y = 2$ **9.** $4x + y = 10$ **10.** $2x + 2y = 20$

_____   _____   _____

_____   _____   _____

MIXED APPLICATIONS

11. The number of hours Julie practices her violin each week, y, is 3 hr more than the number of hours she studies, x. Write an equation to show the relationship of the two activities.

_____

12. Mark spends double the amount of time reading as he does listening to tapes. If he spends 4.5 hr reading and listening to tapes, how long does he spend doing each activity?

_____

EVERYDAY MATH CONNECTION

13. In order to find the number of kilometers in 30 mi, multiply the number of miles by 1.6 km. If x is the number of miles and y is the number of kilometers, this is the equation: $y = 1.6x$. There are 48 km in 30 mi: $48 = 1.6 \cdot 30$. Using the formula, find how many kilometers are there in 40 mi.

_____

Graphing Equations

Use the graph of $y = x + 2$ for Exercises 1–4.

1. What is the solution of the equation at point A?

_____

2. What is the solution of the equation at point B?

_____

3. What is the value of x when the value of y is 2?

_____

4. What is another solution of $y = x + 2$?

_____

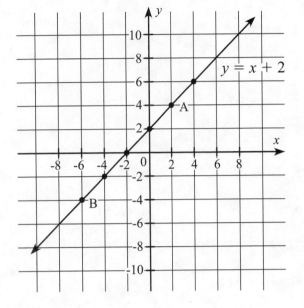

Graph the equations on a piece of graph paper. Use at least three ordered pairs.

5. $y = x - 2$ 6. $y = 2x + 1$ 7. $y = x + 5$ 8. $y = 3x$

MIXED APPLICATIONS

9. Stacey studies twice as long as Kathy. Write an equation to find the number of hours Stacey studies, y, when Kathy studies x hours. Graph the equation.

_____

10. Use the graph in Exercise 9 to find how many hours Stacey studies when Kathy studies 4 hr.

_____

LOGICAL REASONING

13. Since the graph of $y = x + 2$ is a straight line, how many solutions to the equation do you think there are?

_____

Linear Functions

Determine which of the given points lies on the graph of the given function. Circle a, b, or c for all that apply.

1. $x - 5y = 6$ **a.** $(11, 1)$ **b.** $(4, -2)$ **c.** $(1, -1)$

2. $3x - y = 8$ **a.** $(3, 0)$ **b.** $(-2, -2)$ **c.** $(4, 4)$

3. $y = -2x + 4$ **a.** $(1, 2)$ **b.** $(0, -4)$ **c.** $(2, 0)$

4. $3x + 2y = 12$ **a.** $(3, 2)$ **b.** $(2, 3)$ **c.** $(4, 0)$

5. $2x + 2y = 20$ **a.** $(2, 8)$ **b.** $(1, 6)$ **c.** $(6, 4)$

6. $y = 2x + 3$ **a.** $(3, 9)$ **b.** $(2, 7)$ **c.** $(8, 19)$

7. $y = \frac{3}{4}x + 3$ **a.** $(9, 6)$ **b.** $(0, 4)$ **c.** $(4, 6)$

8. $-4y = 3x - 12$ **a.** $(3, \frac{3}{4})$ **b.** $(6, 7.5)$ **c.** $(9, -3)$

9. $y = -x$ **a.** $(4, -8)$ **b.** $(10, -10)$ **c.** $(12, -12)$

10. $y = 5x - 3$ **a.** $(2, 7)$ **b.** $(0, -3)$ **c.** $(5, 22)$

11. $y = \frac{2}{3}x + 2$ **a.** $(3, 4)$ **b.** $(6, 0)$ **c.** $(9, 10)$

MIXED REVIEW

Make a mapping diagram to represent the ordered pairs of each of the relations.

12.

x	y
1	5
2	7
3	9
4	11
5	13

13.

x	y
4	2
4	-2
16	4
16	-4
25	5
25	-5

Name _____   Date _____

Slope

Identify the slope of each line. Write whether the slope is *positive* or *negative*.

1.
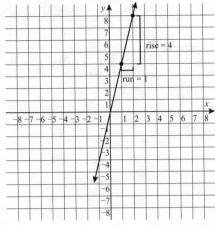

_____   _____

2.
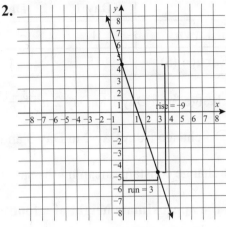

_____   _____

3.
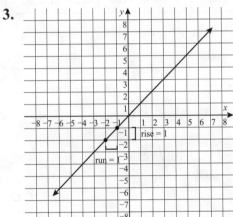

4.
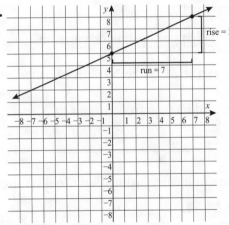

_____   _____

5.
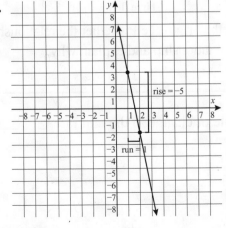

6.
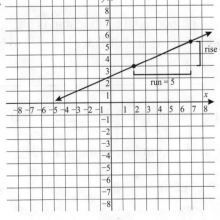

_____   _____

77

Name _____ Date _____

Rate of Change and Slope

Eve keeps a record of the number of lawns she mows and the money she earns.

	Day 1	Day 2	Day 3	Day 4	Day 5
Number of Lawns	1	3	6	8	13
Amount Earned ($)	15	45	90	120	195

1. The rate of change from Day 1 to Day 2 is $\frac{45-15}{3-1}$. What is the rate of change? _____

2. Find the rate of change from Day 2 to Day 3 and from Day 4 to Day 5. _____ _____

3. Is the rate of change constant, meaning the same, or variable, meaning different? _____

The table shows the approximate height of a football after it is kicked.

4. Find each rate of change.

   _____

Time (s)	0	0.5	1.5	2
Height (ft)	0	18	31	26

5. Is the rate of change constant or variable? _____

The graph shows the distance Nathan bicycled over time.

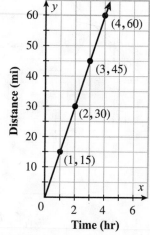

6. Find the rate of change from 1 hour to 2 hours.

   _____

7. Find the rate of change from 1 hour to 4 hours.

   _____

8. The graph of a proportional relationship is a straight line through the origin. Tell whether the relationship between Nathan's time and distance appears to be a proportional relationship and explain why.

   _____

9. What is Nathan's unit rate? _____   10. Compare the rate of change to the unit rate. _____

11. What is the slope of the line in the graph? _____

Complete. Use < , > , or =.

12. slope of line ⃝ rate of change ⃝ unit rate

78

Investigating Slope

The graph shows the linear function $y = -\frac{2}{3}x + 4$.

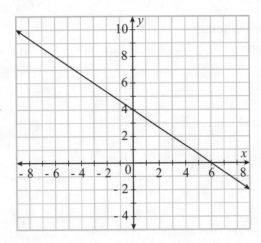

1. Find the slope of the line using the points (0, 4) and (-3, 6).

   _____

2. Find the slope of the line using a different pair of points on the line.

   _____

3. Find the slope of the line using another pair of points on the line.

   _____

4. What does slope represent?

   _____

5. Does it matter which pair of points you use when finding the slope of a line? Explain.

   _____

   _____

Applications of Slope

Erica walks to her friend Philip's house at a constant pace.
The graph shows Erica's distance from home over time.

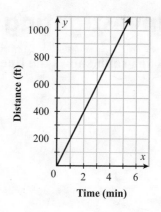

1. Without calculating slope, tell whether
   the slope is positive or negative.

   _____

2. Find the slope of the line. _____

3. Does the value of r in the point $(1, r)$ correspond
   to Erica's unit rate? Explain.

   _____

4. What are the rate of change and the slope of the
   line shown in this graph?

   _____

Plant Growth

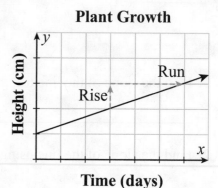

Time (days)

5. What are the rate of change and the slope of
   the line shown in this graph?

   _____

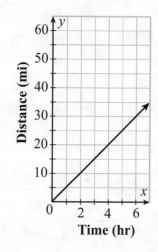

6. What are the rate of change and slope of the
   line shown in this graph?

   _____

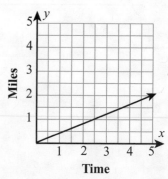

Graphing Functions

Graph the solutions of each equation on a piece of graph paper and tell whether the equation is *linear* or is *not linear*.

1. $y = 3x + 5$

Time (h)	1	3	5	7
Total Amount of Rain (cm)	8	14		

_____

2. $y = x - 5$

Weight (kg), x	1	2	3	4	5
Calories, y					

_____

3. $y = 3x^2 + 5$

Side length, x	1	2	3	4	5
Area, y					

_____

4. $y = 2x + 3$

Input, x	7	8	9	10	11
Output, y					

_____

5. $y = 5 - 2x$

Input, x	-2	-1	0	1	2
Output, y					

_____

6. $y = 2 - x^2$

Input, x	-1	1	3	5
Output, y				

_____

Writing Equations

The U.S. Department of Agriculture defines heavy rain as rain that falls at a rate of 1.5 centimeters per hour.

1. The table shows the total amount of rain that falls in various amounts of time during a heavy rain. Complete the table.

Time (h)	0	1	2	3	4	5
Total Amount of Rain (cm)	0	1.5				

2. Plot the ordered pairs from the table on the coordinate plane at the right.

3. How much rain falls in 3.5 hours?

_____

4. Plot the point corresponding to 3.5 hours of heavy rain.

5. What do you notice about all of the points you plotted?

_____

Experts recommend that adult dogs have a daily intake of 50 calories per kilogram of the dog's weight plus 100 calories.

6. Write an equation that gives the recommended number of daily calories, *y*, for a dog that weighs *x* kilograms.

Daily calories equal 50 times weight plus 100.

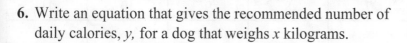

_____ = _____ + _____

7. Complete the table to find some solutions of the equation.

Weight (km), *x*	6	8	10	12	14
Calories, *y*					

8. Plot the points and then draw a line through the points to represent all the possible *x*-values and their corresponding *y*-values.

9. The *x* equation is a linear equation because

_____.

Heavy Rainfall

Recommended Daily Intake

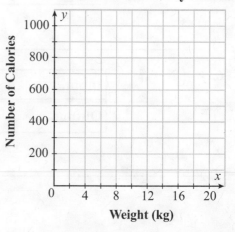

Unit 9
Core Skills Math, Grade 8

Determine Whether an Equation Is Linear

Tell whether each equation is a linear equation.

1. $y = -2x + 1$ _____

2. $y = x^2 + 6$ _____

3. $y = 2x + 3$ _____

4. $y = -x + 6$ _____

5. $y = x^2 - 1$ _____

6. $y = 1 - x$ _____

WRITER'S CORNER

7. A student graphed several solutions of $y = -2x$ as shown. The student concluded that the equation is not a linear equation. Explain the student's error.

_____

_____

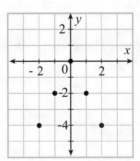

8. A student claims that the equation $y = 7$ is not a linear equation because it does not have the form $y = mx + b$. Do you agree or disagree? Explain your answer.

_____

_____

Slope-Intercept Form

Let (x, y) be a point on line L other than the point containing the y-intercept.

1. Let L be a line with slope m and y-intercept b. Circle the point, or points, that must be on the line. Explain your answer.

   $(b, 0)$ $(0, b)$ $(0, m)$ $(m, 0)$

2. Write an expression for the change in y values between the point that includes the y-intercept and the point (x, y).

   _____

3. Write an expression for the change in x values between the point that includes the y-intercept and the point (x, y).

   _____

4. Using your answers from Exercises 2–3, complete the equation for the slope m of the line.

   $$m = \frac{y - \boxed{}}{\boxed{} - 0}$$

5. Solve the equation from Exercise 4 for y. _____

6. Write the equation of a line with slope m that passes through the origin.

   _____

Write an equation for the line with the given slope and y-intercept.

7. slope: -4; y-intercept: 6

   _____

8. slope: $\frac{5}{2}$; y-intercept: -3

   _____

Graph Using Slope-Intercept Form

1. Graph $y = -2x + 5$.

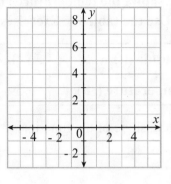

Step 1 Identify the slope and the y-intercept.

slope: $m =$ _____ $= \dfrac{\Box}{1}$

y-intercept: $b =$ _____

Step 2 The point that contains the y-intercept

is (0, _____). Plot this point.

Step 3 Use the slope to find a second point on the line.

Count down _____ unit(s) and

right _____ unit(s). Plot this point.

Step 4 Draw a line connecting the two points.

Graph each equation.

2. $y = \dfrac{1}{2}x + 1$

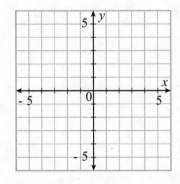

3. $y = -3x + 4$

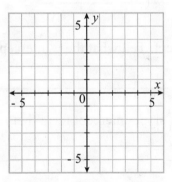

Graph each equation. Then identify the slope and y-intercept of each graph.

4. $7x + 4y = 24$ _____

5. $y = \dfrac{7}{8}x - 4$ _____

6. $6x + 3y = 36$ _____

7. $5x + 8y = 40$ _____

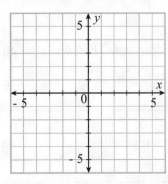

Writing Equations to Describe Functions

The table shows the temperature at different altitudes. The temperature is a linear function of the altitude. Use the table for Exercises 1–4.

Altitude (ft), x	0	2,000	4,000	6,000	8.000	10,000	12,000
Temperature (°F), y	59	51	43	35	27	19	11

1. Find the slope of the function.

_____

2. Find the y-intercept of the function.

_____

3. Write an equation in slope-intercept form that represents the function.

_____

4. Use your equation to determine the temperature at an altitude of 5,000 feet.

_____

The graph shows a scuba diver's ascent over time. Use the graph for Exercises 5 and 6.

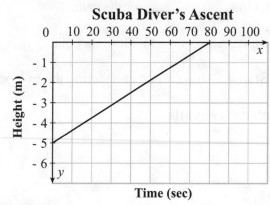

Scuba Diver's Ascent

5. Use the graph to find the slope of the line. Tell what the slope means in this context.

_____

6. Identify the y-intercept. Tell what the y-intercept means in this context.

_____

7. Write an equation in slope-intercept form that represents the function.

_____

The formula for converting Celsius temperatures to Fahrenheit temperatures is a linear function. Water freezes at 0°C, or 32°F, and it boils at 100°C, or 212°F. Use this information for Exercises 8 and 9.

8 Find the slope and y-intercept. Then write an equation in slope-intercept form that represents the function.

_____

9 Average human body temperature is 37°C. What is this temperature in degrees Fahrenheit?

_____

Comparing Functions

The table and the graph display two different linear functions. Use the table and graph for Exercises 1–4.

Input x	Output y
-3	5
-1	1
2	-5
3	-7
6	-13

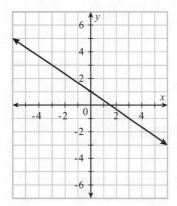

1. Find the slope of each function.

   Table: _____   Graph: _____

2. Without graphing the function represented in the table, tell which function's graph is steeper.

   _____

   _____

3. Write an equation for each function.

   Table: _____   Graph: _____

4. Use the equations from 3 to tell which function has the greater y-intercept.

   _____

5. Find the y-value for each function when $x = 1$.

   Table: _____   Graph: _____

6. Find the y-value for each function when $x = -2$.

   Table: _____   Graph: _____

Exploring Systems of Equations

Graph each set of equations on graph paper and find the point of intersection.

1. $y = x - 2$

$y = -x$

_____

2. $y = x + 4$

$y = 6 - x$

_____

3. $y = 2x - 2$

$y = 4x$

_____

MIXED APPLICATIONS

Write a system of equations for Exercises 4 and 5. Solve each system by graphing.

4. John and Mark studied a total of 15 hr. Mark studied 3 more hours than John. How many hours did each study?

_____

5. Jody exercised a total of 18 hr last week. She spent twice as much time jogging as doing sit-ups. How much time did she spend on each?

_____

MIXED REVIEW

Compute.

6. $\frac{3}{2} + \frac{7}{2}$ _____

7. $\frac{3}{4} + \frac{5}{2}$ _____

8. $\frac{3}{10} + \frac{4}{5}$ _____

9. $\frac{4}{5} - \frac{2}{5}$ _____

10. $\frac{3}{9} - \frac{5}{3}$ _____

11. $\frac{32}{21} - \frac{5}{7}$ _____

12. $\frac{6}{9} \times \frac{1}{3}$ _____

13. $\frac{7}{2} \times \frac{10}{3}$ _____

14. $\frac{20}{13} \times \frac{11}{2}$ _____

15. $\frac{4}{9} \div \frac{5}{12}$ _____

16. $\frac{6}{11} \div \frac{7}{2}$ _____

17. $\frac{1}{9} \div \frac{3}{8}$ _____

90

Name _____ Date _____

Solving Systems of Equations Graphically

Solve each system by graphing.

1. $\begin{cases} 2x - 4y = 10 \\ x + y = 2 \end{cases}$ _____

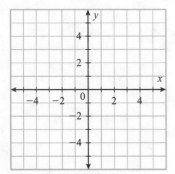

2. $\begin{cases} 2x - y = 0 \\ x + y = -6 \end{cases}$ _____

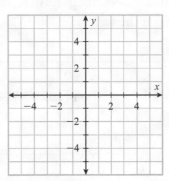

Graph each system and tell how many solutions the system has.

3. $\begin{cases} x - 3y = 2 \\ -3x + 9y = -6 \end{cases}$

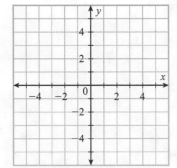

_____ solutions

4. $\begin{cases} 2x - y = 5 \\ 2x - y = -1 \end{cases}$

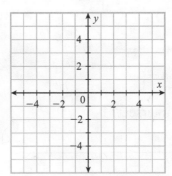

_____ solutions

Name _____ Date _____

Applications of Systems of Equations

Mrs. Morales wrote a test with 15 questions covering spelling and vocabulary. Spelling questions (x) are worth 5 points and vocabulary questions (y) are worth 10 points. The maximum number of points possible on the test is 100. Use this information for Exercises 1–4.

1. Write an equation in slope-intercept form to represent the number of questions on the test.

   _____

2. Write an equation in slope-intercept form to represent the total points on the test.

   _____

3. Graph the solutions of both equations.

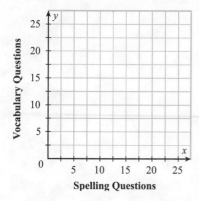

4. Where do the lines intersect?

   _____

5. Use your graph to tell how many of each question type are on the test.

   _____ spelling questions; _____ vocabulary questions

Solving Systems of Equations Algebraically

Solve each system of equations algebraically.

1. $\begin{cases} y = \frac{2}{3}x - 5 \\ y = -x + 10 \end{cases}$

2. $\begin{cases} 3x + 2y = 9 \\ y = 4x - 1 \end{cases}$

3. $\begin{cases} 5x - 2y = 4 \\ 2x - y = 1 \end{cases}$

_____   _____   _____

4. $\begin{cases} 2x + y = 9 \\ 3x - y = 16 \end{cases}$

5. $\begin{cases} 2y = 3x - 2 \\ y = 2x + 1 \end{cases}$

6. $\begin{cases} y = 2x + 1 \\ 3y = 18x + 15 \end{cases}$

_____   _____   _____

7. $\begin{cases} y = 4x + 2 \\ 3y = 9x + 18 \end{cases}$

8. $\begin{cases} y = 3x + 2 \\ y = 5x - 10 \end{cases}$

_____   _____

LOGICAL REASONING

9. Zach solves the system $\begin{cases} x + y = -3 \\ x - y = 1 \end{cases}$ and finds the solution $(1, -2)$.

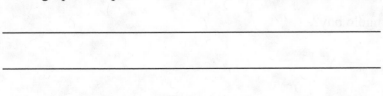

Use a graph to explain whether Zach's solution is reasonable.

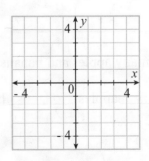

_____

_____

_____

93

Problem Solving with Systems of Equations

1. Angelica solves the system $\begin{cases} 3x - y = 0 \\ \frac{1}{4}x + \frac{3}{4}y = \frac{5}{2} \end{cases}$

and finds the solution (1, 3). Use substitution to explain why Angelica's solution is correct.

_____

Angelo bought apples and bananas at the fruit stand. He bought 20 pieces of fruit and spent $11.50. Apples cost $0.50 and bananas cost $0.75 each. Use this information for Exercises 2–5.

2. Write an equation to represent the number of pieces of fruit.

_____

3. Write an equation to represent the money spent on the fruit.

_____

4. Solve the system algebraically.

_____

5. How many apples and bananas did Angelo buy?

_____ apples; _____ bananas

Name _____   Date _____

Problem-Solving Strategy

GUESS AND CHECK

Solve.

1. Tickets for the school play cost $6.00 for adults and $3.50 for students. Mark paid $13.00 for fewer than 3 tickets of each type. How many adult tickets and how many student tickets did Mark buy?

   _____

2. Judy sold some records for $1.00 each and some tapes for $1.50 each. She sold fewer than 5 of each type and collected $8.50 in all. How many of each did she sell?

   _____

3. Andy delivers the local paper at $0.55 each and the city paper at $1.10 each. He delivered fewer than 5 papers of each type and collected $4.40. How many of each type did he deliver?

   _____

4. Joan bought some pencils for $0.15 each and some pens for $0.35 each. She has fewer than 7 in all. How many pens and how many pencils did she buy for $1.50?

   _____

MIXED APPLICATIONS

Solve.

5. The school newspaper club published 20,000 newspapers. On Monday, the club sold 50% of the newspapers. Each day thereafter, the club sold 20% of the remaining newspapers. How many newspapers were left to sell after Friday?

   _____

6. At a soccer game, the students sold sandwiches for $1.00 each and juice containers for $0.75 each. How many sandwiches and how many containers of juice did they sell if they made $16.75? Give all possible combinations.

   _____

   _____

   _____

LOGICAL REASONING

7. The local theater seats 102 people. At the play on Friday night, there was one empty seat for every two occupied seats. How many people were at the play?

   _____

Frequency Tables and Histograms

1. Make a side-by-side frequency table and a side-by-side histogram for the geography test scores.

Geography Test Scores					
Boys			Girls		
25	32	26	27	35	39
40	39	28	28	24	21

Boys			Girls	
Tally	Frequency	Score	Frequency	Tally
		36-40		
		31-35		
		26-30		
		21-25		

Geography Test Scores				
Boys		Scores	Girls	
		36-40		
		31-35		
		26-30		
		21-25		

2. What is the range of scores for girls? boys?

_____

3. How many students have scores in the interval 36-40?

_____

Use the histogram to answer Exercises 4 and 5.

4. Did more men or more women use the library on Monday evening?

_____

5. How many people under 21 years of age used the library on Monday evening?

_____

Monday Evening Library Users		
Men	Ages	Women
	51 and over	
	41-50	
	31-40	
	21-30	
	11-20	
12 10 8 6 4 2		2 4 6 8 10

SOCIAL STUDIES CONNECTION

6. Find a graph on the Internet, in a newspaper, or some other source. Decide whether the data in that graph could have been presented in a histogram. Explain.

_____

96

Line Graphs

1. Choose the graph that represents this situation. Circle *a*, *b*, or *c*. You are driving at 25 miles per hour. After some time you increase your speed to the speed limit and maintain that speed. Then you slow down to 25 miles per hour.

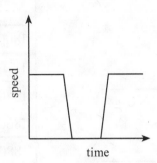

a.   b.   c.

2. Construct a double-line graph for the data in the following table.

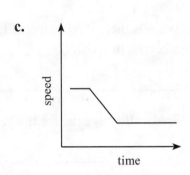

Average Monthly Precipitation (in inches)						
	Jan.	Feb.	March	April	May	June
Morgantown	0.7	0.8	0.7	0.6	1.0	1.1
Lowell	3.2	2.7	1.6	0.5	0.5	0.5

Use the data and your line graph to answer Exercises 3 and 4.

3. What is the total rainfall for January through June for Morgantown?

_____

4. Which town has a more consistent amount of rainfall?

_____

WRITER'S CORNER

5. Describe a school-related situation for which a double-line graph would be a good way to present the data.

_____

_____

_____

Name _____ Date _____

Making Inferences

Display the Cook Corporation data in a line graph. Then use the table and graph for Exercises 1–6.

1. What is the trend for the data?

   _____

2. What is the interpolation of the revenue received in 1870?

   _____

3. Predict the revenue for the year 2000.

   _____

4. What is the increase in the revenue between 1900 and 1960?

   _____

5. What might the revenue have been for 1970?

   _____

6. What is the average revenue for the years given?

   _____

Cook Corporation Revenue			
Year	Revenue (in millions)	Year	Revenue (in millions)
1800	$6.2	1900	$75
1820	$8.9	1920	$107
1840	$16	1940	$133
1860	$30	1960	$180
1880	$50	1980	$230

SOCIAL STUDIES CONNECTION

7. Use the Internet or a reference book to research some of the different types of statistics that the U.S. government keeps on population. List some of these statistics and tell how you think they are used.

   _____

   _____

Unit 11
Core Skills Math, Grade 8

Two-Way Tables

Karen asked 150 students at her school if they played sports. She also recorded whether the student was a boy or girl. Of the 150 students, 20% did not play sports, 60% of the total were girls, and 70% of the girls played sports. Use the table for Exercises 1–4.

	Sports	No Sports	TOTAL
Boys			
Girls			
TOTAL			

1. Complete the two-way table.

2. What is the relative frequency of a student playing sports? _____

3. What is the relative frequency of a boy playing sports? _____

4. Is there an association between being a boy and playing sports at Karen's school? Explain.

_____

_____

_____

Aiden collected data from 80 students about whether they have siblings and whether they have pets. Use the table for Exercises 5–7.

	Siblings	No Siblings	TOTAL
Pets	49	21	70
No Pets	7	3	10
TOTAL	56	24	80

5. What is the relative frequency of a student having pets? _____

6. What is the relative frequency of a student with siblings having pets? _____

7. Is there an association between having siblings and having pets? Explain.

_____

_____

_____

Making a Scatter Plot

The final question on a math test reads, "How many hours did you spend studying for this test?" The teacher records the number of hours each student studied and the grade the student received on the test.

Hours Spent Studying	Test Grade
0	75
0.5	80
1	80
1	85
1.5	85
1.5	95
2	90
3	100
4	90

1. Make a prediction about the relationship between the number of hours spent studying and test grades.

_____

_____

_____

2. Make a scatter plot. Graph hours spent studying as the independent variable and test grade as the dependent variable.

3. What trend do you see in the data?

_____

_____

_____

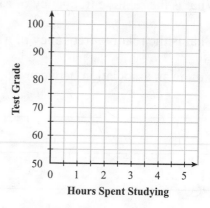

4. Do you think that studying for 10 hours would greatly increase a student's grade?

_____

_____

5. Why might a student who studied fewer hours make a higher score?

_____

_____

100

Interpreting Clusters and Outliers

A scientist gathers information about the eruptions of Old Faithful, a geyser in Yellowstone National Park. She uses the data to create a scatter plot. The data show the length of time between eruptions (interval) and how long the eruption lasts (duration).

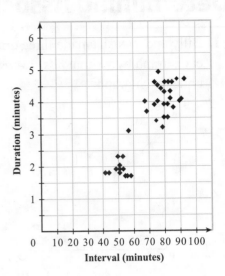

1. Describe any clusters you see in the scatter plot.

_____

_____

2. What do the clusters tell you about eruptions of Old Faithful?

_____

_____

3. Describe any outliers you see in the scatter plot.

_____

_____

4. Suppose the geyser erupts for 2.2 minutes after a 75-minute interval. Would this point lie in one of the clusters? Would it be an outlier? Explain your answer.

_____

_____

_____

5. Suppose the geyser erupts after an 80-minute interval. Give a range of possible duration times for which the point on the scatter plot would not be considered an outlier. Give your reasoning.

_____

_____

_____

© Houghton Mifflin Harcourt Publishing Company

Determining Association

1. Billy and Tanisha made three graphs for data they collected as part of a school project. Label each graph by writing *positive association*, *negative association*, or *no association* on the line under each graph.

a.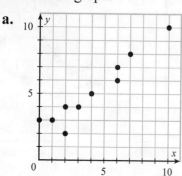

b.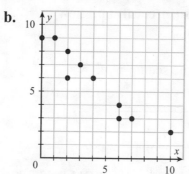

c.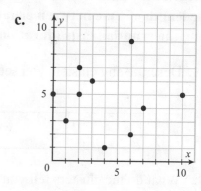

_____   _____   _____

Susan surveyed 20 people about the price of a cleaning product she developed. She asked each person whether they would buy the cleaner at different prices. A person may answer yes or no to more than one price. Susan's results are shown in the table. Use this information for Exercises 2 and 3.

Price ($)	Buyers
2	20
4	19
6	17
8	13
10	8
12	2

2. Make a scatter plot of the data on this graph.

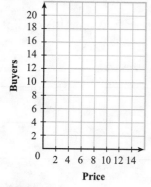

3. Describe the type(s) of association you see between price and number of people who would buy at that price. Explain.

_____

_____

Name _____   Date _____

Drawing a Trend Line

Joyce is training for a 10K race. For some of her training runs, she records the distance she ran and how many minutes she ran. Use this information for Exercises 1–4.

Distance (mi)	Time (min)
4	38
2	25
1	7
2	16
3	26
5	55
2	20
4	45
3	31

1. Make a scatter plot of Joyce's running data on this graph.

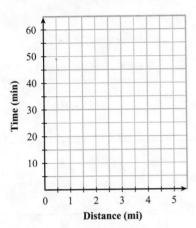

2. Draw a trend line using a straightedge. When you draw the line, make sure there are about the same number of points above and below it.

3. Use your trend line to predict how long it would take Joyce to run 4.5 miles.

_____

4. How well does your trend line fit the data?

_____

Use the scatter plot for Exercises 5 and 6.

5. If you draw a trend line, will all the points be close to the line? Explain your answer.

_____

_____

6. Draw the trend line and use it to predict the depth of the water at 17 minutes.

_____

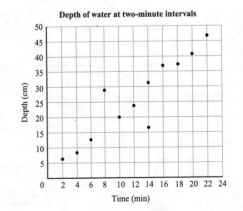

Depth of water at two-minute intervals

Name _____ Date _____

Using a Linear Model

The scatter plot shows the relationship between the number of chapters and the total number of pages for several books. Use the scatter plot for Exercises 1–7.

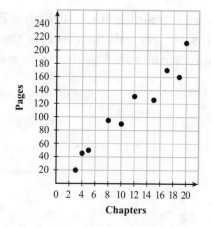

1. Draw a trend line. (Hint: Use (5, 50) as one of the points.)

   Identify another point that the trend line goes through:

   (_____, _____).

2. What type(s) of association does the scatter plot show?

   _____

3. Do you expect the slope of the line to be positive or negative?

   _____

4. Find the slope of the trend line.

   $$m = \frac{\boxed{} - 50}{\boxed{} - 5} = \frac{\boxed{}}{\boxed{}} = \underline{\quad}$$

5. Use the equation $y = mx + b$, the slope, and the point (5, 50) to solve for b.

   _____

6. What is the equation of the trend line?

   _____

7. What is the meaning of the slope in this situation?

   _____

   _____

LOGICAL REASONING

8. A scatter plot shows the relationship between a baby's length and age. Why might an extrapolated data point not be very accurate?

   _____

   _____

Probability

You spin the spinner. Find each probability.

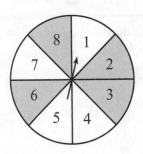

1. p(2) _____

2. p(not 4) _____

3. p(3 or 2) _____

4. p(1, 4, or 5) _____

5. p(5 or gray) _____

6. p(5 or white) _____

You roll a number cube numbered from 1 to 6. Find each probability.

7. p(5) _____

8. p(3 or 4) _____

9. p(not 5) _____

10. p(number > 3) _____

11. p(odd number) _____

12. p(number < 1) _____

13. What is the sample space when you flip three coins?

_____

MIXED APPLICATIONS

14. If you throw a cube numbered 1–6, an even number gets you a prize. What is the probability that you will win a prize on a throw?

_____

15. Free science catalogs are being distributed. They have an equal number of blue, green, red, or orange covers. What is the probability that the catalog you receive will have a green cover?

_____

MIXED REVIEW

Write each fraction in simplest form.

16. $\frac{12}{15}$ _____

17. $\frac{24}{15}$ _____

18. $\frac{35}{50}$ _____

19. $\frac{18}{81}$ _____

Compute.

20. $\frac{4 \times 2}{3 \times 2}$ = _____

21. $\frac{5 \times 6 \times 7}{1 \times 2 \times 3}$ = _____

22. $\frac{12 \times 10 \times 9}{60}$ = _____

Exploring Pascal's Triangle

1. Complete Pascal's Triangle.

Row 0   1

Row 1   1   +   1

Row 2   1   _____   1

Row 3   1   _____   _____   1

Row 4   1   _____   _____   _____   1

You toss 4 coins. Find each probability. Use the numbers and their sum from Row 4 of Pascal's Triangle.

2. p(4 heads) _____   **3.** p(4 tails) _____   **4.** p(3 tails) _____

You toss 5 coins. Find each probability.

5. p(5 heads) _____   **6.** p(5 tails) _____   **7.** p(4 heads) _____

Use Pascal's Triangle for Exercises 8 and 9.

8. Complete Row 5 and give its elements.   **9.** Complete Row 6 and give its elements.

_____   _____

Use Pascal's Triangle.

10. Find the sum of the numbers in each of Rows 0–5.

_____

11. Give the second element in Row 8.

_____

WRITER'S CORNER

12. Explain how to find the numbers for a row of Pascal's Triangle using the numbers in the row above.

_____

_____

106

Problem-Solving Strategy

USE A DIAGRAM

Use Pascal's Triangle to solve.

1. A yacht club with 10 members wants to elect 4 officers. How many combinations of 4 officers can be elected from the 10 members?

   _____

2. Two students in an eighth grade-class with 12 students will win an award. In how many ways can 2 winners be chosen from 12 students?

   _____

3. There are 9 members of the art club, but only 3 of them may go to an art exhibition. In how many ways can the three persons be selected?

   _____

4. The bicycle shop has 10 models of bicycles. Of these, 6 will be displayed in the window. In how many ways can the selection be made?

   _____

MIXED APPLICATIONS

Solve.

5. Noel is arranging 10 books on a shelf. In how many ways can the books be placed?

   _____

6. Mara earned $3,000. If she repaid a loan of $500 with 10% interest, how much money did she have left?

   _____

7. Tai drove 200 miles in $3\frac{1}{2}$ hours. What was his average speed to the nearest whole number?

   _____

8. A bus traveled for $2\frac{2}{3}$ hr at a speed of 55 mph. How far did the bus travel?

   _____

MIXED REVIEW

Solve for x.

9. $x + 3 = \frac{210}{7}$

   _____

10. $5x - 10 = \frac{80}{2}$

    _____

11. $4.5x = 68.4$

    _____

Random Numbers

The random numbers 0–9 in the table were generated by a computer. Use the table for Exercises 1–4.

50 Random Numbers									
1	2	4	5	8	7	3	5	7	9
3	5	7	2	6	9	4	7	2	0
2	6	0	7	4	2	7	8	3	8
2	6	5	4	8	0	9	2	5	6
2	8	7	4	5	0	8	9	2	3

1. You are playing a game using the spinner shown. Use the table to simulate 50 spins. How many spins will it take before you get all the numbers from 0–9?

_____

2. Use the spinner again with the table. How many spins will it take to get number 7 twice?

_____

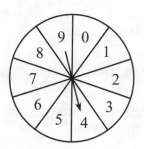

3. Using the theoretical probability, predict how many times the spinner will stop on 5 if you spin 40 times.

_____

4. What is the probability of getting number 3 in 10 spins? Use the data from the table.

_____

MIXED APPLICATIONS

5. Jean put 10 cards numbered 0–9 in a bag. Amy takes a card out and puts it back. Predict the number of times Amy will pick the 2-card if she picks 50 times.

6. José went to buy car tires. Each tire cost him $30. If he wanted to change all of his 4 tires, how much would it cost him?

WRITER'S CORNER

7. Computer programmers often use random numbers in writing many different kinds of programs. Describe two kinds of programs in which random numbers might be useful.

_____

_____

108

Similar and Congruent Figures

On each grid, draw a polygon similar to the one shown and a polygon congruent to the one shown.

1.
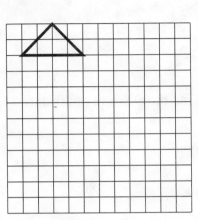

2.
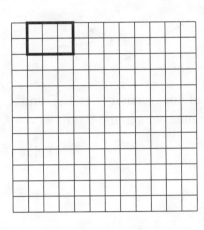

3.
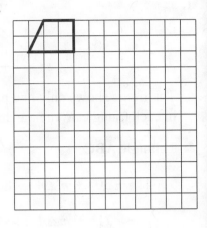

4.
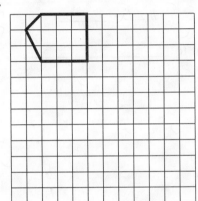

5.
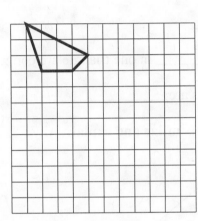

6.
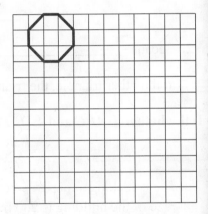

MIXED APPLICATIONS

7. How many square pieces of construction paper, each 4 cm on a side, do you need to cover a square piece of paper that measures 40 cm on a side?

_____

8. Marilee has 2 cups. The cups are similar, but not congruent. Can Marilee store one cup inside the other cup? Explain your answer.

_____

_____

LOGICAL REASONING

9. Are congruent figures similar? Explain your answer.

_____

Proving Triangles Are Similar

Tell whether the triangles are similar and explain why.

1.

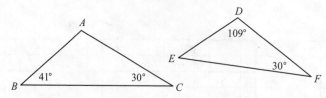

The figure shows only one pair of congruent angles, $\angle C$ and $\angle F$. Find the measure of the third angle in each triangle. Write the angle measures in the figure.

Triangle ABC

$$41° + 30° + m\angle A = 180°$$

$$71° + m\angle A = 180°$$

$$m\angle A = \underline{\hspace{1cm}}$$

Triangle DEF

$$\underline{\hspace{1cm}} + \underline{\hspace{1cm}} + m\angle E = 180°$$

$$\underline{\hspace{1cm}} + m\angle E = 180°$$

$$m\angle E = \underline{\hspace{1cm}}$$

2. Because _____ in one triangle are congruent to _____

in the other triangle, the triangles are _____.

Tell whether △ABC and △DEF are similar and explain why.

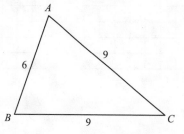

3. Corresponding parts of triangles are listed in the same order, so $\overline{AB}$ corresponds

to $\overline{DE}$, $\overline{BC}$ corresponds to _____, and $\overline{AC}$ corresponds to _____.

4. Determine whether the lengths of corresponding sides are proportional.

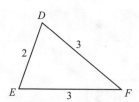   *Substitute the lengths from the figure.*

$\overline{AC}$ is congruent to $\overline{BC}$ and $\overline{DF}$ is congruent to $\overline{EF}$, so you do not need to set up a second proportion.

Because the lengths of corresponding sides are _____, the triangles

are _____.

114

Similar Triangles

1. Two transversals intersect two parallel lines as shown.
Tell whether △ABC and △DEC are similar and explain why.

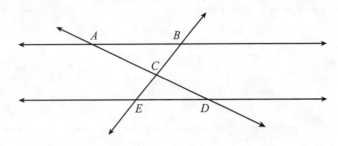

_____

_____

_____

2. A flagpole casts a shadow 23.5 feet long. At the same time of day, Mrs. Gilbert, who is 5.5 feet tall, casts a shadow that is 7.5 feet long. Write a proportion that can be used to solve the problem. How tall in feet is the flagpole? Round your answer to the tenths place.

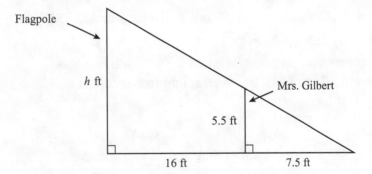

Flagpole

h ft

Mrs. Gilbert

5.5 ft

16 ft   7.5 ft

3. △LMN and △QRS are similar. Find the value of x.

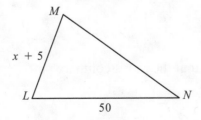

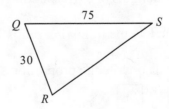

$x + 5$

50

75

30

Using Similar Triangles to Explain Slope

Use similar triangles to show that the slope of a line is constant.
Use this space to make your drawing:

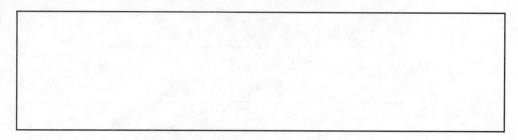

1. Draw line ℓ that is not a horizontal line. Label four points on the line as *A*, *B*, *C*, and *D*. You need to show that the slope between points *A* and *B* is the same as the slope between points *C* and *D*.

2. Draw the rise and run for the slope between points *A* and *B*. Label the intersection as point *E*. Draw the rise and run for the slope between points *C* and *D*. Label the intersection as point *F*.

3. Write expressions for the slope between *A* and *B* and between *C* and *D*.

   Slope between *A* and *B*: $\dfrac{BE}{\boxed{}}$ Slope between *C* and *D*: $\dfrac{\boxed{}}{CF}$

4. Extend $\overleftrightarrow{AE}$ and $\overleftrightarrow{CF}$ across your drawing. $\overleftrightarrow{AE}$ and $\overleftrightarrow{CF}$ are both horizontal lines, so they are parallel. Line ℓ is a transversal that intersects parallel lines.

5. Complete the following statements:

   ∠*BAE* and _____ are corresponding angles and are _____.

   ∠*BEA* and _____ are right angles and are _____.

6. By Angle-Angle Similarity, △*ABE* and _____ are similar triangles.

7. Use the fact that the lengths of corresponding sides of similar triangles are proportional to complete the following ratios $\dfrac{BE}{DF} = \dfrac{\boxed{}}{CF}$.

8. Recall that you can also write the proportion so that the ratios compare parts of the same triangle: $\dfrac{\boxed{}}{AE} = \dfrac{DF}{\boxed{}}$.

9. The proportion you wrote in Exercise 8 shows that the ratios you wrote in Exercise 3 are equal. So, the slope of the line is _____.

Exploring Circles

Name the polygon formed when chords connect adjacent endpoints of the arcs. Find each arc measure in degrees.

1.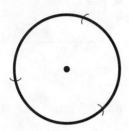

_____

2.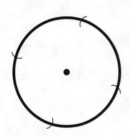

_____

3.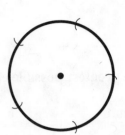

_____

4.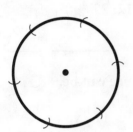

_____

5.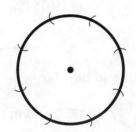

_____

6.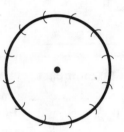

_____

MIXED APPLICATIONS

Use the figure for Exercises 7–9. $\overleftrightarrow{AB} \parallel \overleftrightarrow{MN}$.

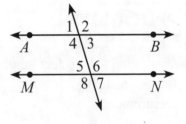

7. Name two pairs of corresponding angles.

_____

8. Suppose m∠5 = 60°. What is m∠6? Explain how you found the measure.

_____

9. If the transversal were perpendicular to $\overleftrightarrow{AB}$, what would be true of the alternate interior and exterior angles?

_____

MIXED REVIEW

Multiply or divide. Write each answer in simplest form.

10. $\frac{3}{5} \times \frac{9}{4}$ _____

11. $8 \div \frac{4}{5}$ _____

12. $\frac{9}{14} \div 1$ _____

13. $\frac{1}{3} \times \frac{15}{19}$ _____

14. $\frac{3}{8} \div \frac{6}{11}$ _____

15. $\frac{1}{2} \times \frac{6}{15}$ _____

16. $\frac{9}{10} \times \frac{5}{8}$ _____

17. $\frac{14}{15} \div 2$ _____

Unit 13
Core Skills Math, Grade 8

Precision: Greatest Possible Error

Name _____ Date _____

Give the precision of each measurement.

1. 9 m

2. $4\frac{1}{4}$ ft

3. $7\frac{1}{8}$ in.

4. 3.4 km

_____ _____ _____ _____

Find the greatest possible error of each measurement.

5. 65 mm

6. 23 yd

7. 7.5 m

8. 7.85 km

_____ _____ _____ _____

9. $170\frac{1}{4}$ ft

10. $3\frac{1}{3}$ mi

11. 0.354 m

12. $23\frac{3}{16}$ ft

_____ _____ _____ _____

For each given measurement, tell how small and how large the actual measure can be.

13. 50 mi

14. 60 mm

15. 34.5 km

16. $11\frac{1}{2}$ yd

_____ _____ _____ _____

MIXED APPLICATIONS

17. A shark was found to be 6 feet long. What is the greatest possible error of this measurement?

_____

18. The swimming pool in the gym is 12 ft deep. Find the largest and smallest value for the actual depth.

_____

WRITER'S CORNER

19. There are more than 15,000 kinds of books in the library. The smallest are science manuals with a width of 14 cm. The largest are atlases with a width of 36 cm. Write a question using this information.

_____

_____

_____

Exploring Significant Digits

Find the appropriate number of significant digits for each answer.

1. $1 + 3.2$

2. $12.3 - 10.34$

3. 2.1×1.38

_____   _____   _____

Find each sum or difference. Use rounding to express the answer with the correct number of significant digits.

4. $16.87 + 13$

5. $20.324 - 10.1$

6. $3.28 + 7.354$

_____   _____   _____

Find each product. Use rounding to express the answer with the correct number of significant digits.

7. 2.3×2

8. 3.84×2

9. 3.50×1.1

_____   _____   _____

MIXED APPLICATIONS

10. A boat can carry a load of 1,000 lb (to the nearest pound). How many significant digits does this measure have?

_____

11. A building is 100 ft tall (to the nearest foot). How many significant digits does this height have?

_____

MIXED REVIEW

Write the reciprocal of each number.

12. 4

13. $\frac{1}{7}$

14. $\frac{3}{5}$

15. $\frac{6}{8}$

_____   _____   _____   _____

Find each sum or difference.

16. $1.2 + 3.4$

17. $3.45 - 1.45$

18. $1.234 + 3.450$

_____   _____   _____

Name _____ Date _____

Exploring Surface Area of Cylinders and Cones

Complete each formula for surface area.

1. $S_{cone} = \pi r^2 +$ _____

2. $S_{cylinder} =$ _____ $\pi r^2 +$ _____ πr _____

3. Find the surface area of a cone with 5 cm slant height and a 3 cm radius. _____

Find the surface area of each figure. Use $\pi = 3.14$. Round to the nearest tenth.

4.
_____

5.
_____

6.
_____

7.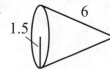
_____

8.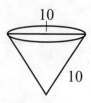
_____

9.
_____

10.
_____

11.
_____

12.
_____

13.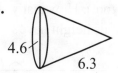
_____

14.
_____

15.
_____

NUMBER SENSE

The words in the box will help you find the numerical
value of π to six decimal places.

16. What is the value of π to 6 decimal places?
(HINT: Count the number of letters in each
word, in sequence.)

_____

Pie.
I wish I could calculate Pie.

Name _____ Date _____

Volume of Cylinders and Cones

Find the volume of each figure. Use π = 3.14 and round to the nearest whole number.

1.

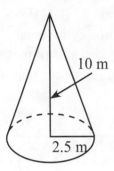

10 m

2.5 m

_____

2.

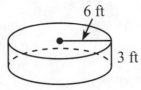

6 ft

3 ft

_____

3.

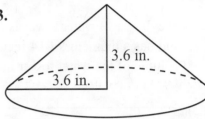

3.6 in.

3.6 in.

_____

Find the volume of the shaded portion. Use π = 3.14 and round to the nearest whole number.

4.

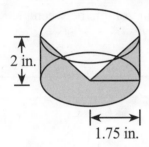

2 in.

1.75 in.

_____

5.

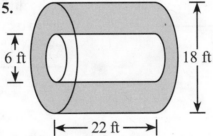

6 ft

18 ft

22 ft

_____

6.

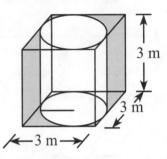

3 m

3 m

3 m

_____

MIXED APPLICATIONS

7. A cone has a radius of 3 m, a height of 4 m, and a slant height of 5 m. What is the volume of the cone?

_____

8. A cylindrical gas tank has a volume of 1,808.64 m³. Its height is 9 m. What is its radius?

_____

MIXED REVIEW

Find each surface area. Round to the nearest tenth.

9. cube with side 3.2 in.

_____

10. square prism with side 2.1 cm; height 4.4 cm

_____

121

Unit 14
Core Skills Math, Grade 8

Formula for Volume of a Cylinder

Solve. Use the formula for volume of a cylinder. Use $\pi = 3.14$.

1. A cylindrical water tower is 60 feet high and has a diameter of 14 feet. What is the volume of the water tower in cubic feet?

_____

2. A tank in the shape of a cylinder is 6 meters wide (diameter) and 14 meters high. What is the volume of the tank in cubic meters?

_____

3. A city water tank has a diameter of 35 feet and a height of 60 feet. How many cubic feet of water will the tank hold?

_____

4. Two cylinders have the same 20 cm height. One has a radius of 7 cm and the other has a radius of 14 cm. What is the difference in volume between the two cylinders?

_____

5. A can has a diameter of 3 inches and is 5 inches high. How many cubic inches will it hold?

_____

6. A coffee can has a diameter of 4 inches and a height of 5.5 inches. How many cubic inches of coffee will it hold?

_____

7. A cylinder has a volume of 141.3 cm³ and a height of 5 cm. What is the radius of the cylinder?

_____

8. A cylinder has a volume of 351.68 m³ and a diameter of 8 m. What is the height of the cylinder?

_____

Problem-Solving Strategy

USE A FORMULA

Use the formula $V = \frac{4}{3}\pi r^3$ for Exercises 1–4.

1. A tennis ball has a diameter of 6.5 cm. A soccer ball has a 22-cm diameter. How many tennis balls would it take to exceed the volume of a soccer ball?

_____

2. Darren's inflated balloon can reach a diameter of 9 cm. If Darren fills his balloon with water, how much will it weigh if $1 \text{ cm}^3 = 1 \text{ g}$?

_____

3. A sphere will fit perfectly in a cube 6 in. on a side. What is the volume of the cube less that of the sphere?

4. How many oranges of radius 4.5 cm will fit in a box 27 cm by 81 cm by 9 cm?

_____

MIXED APPLICATIONS

Solve.

5. Kelly can shovel snow off a 20 ft by 8 ft driveway in 43 min. At the same rate, how long will it take her to shovel a driveway that is 15 ft by 15 ft?

_____

6. Juanita is saving 40% of her weekly earnings to buy a bike. If the bike costs $215, how much must she earn to have enough for the bike?

_____

7. Susan has four times as many pennies as dimes and one-third as many quarters as pennies. If she has 38 coins, how much money does she have?

_____

8. If 12.3 m^3 per minute will flow through a water faucet, about how long will it take to fill a cylinder halfway if the cylinder has a radius 4 meters and a height of 12 meters?

_____

EVERYDAY MATH CONNECTION

9. Jon can carry 25 pounds in the basket of his bicycle. Today's issue of the newspaper has 76 pages and 23 pages in a newspaper weight about 1 pound. If Jon has to deliver papers to 33 different customers, how many trips must Jon make to pick up the papers he is going to deliver?

_____

Interior Angles

1. Two angles in a triangle are 72° and 65°. Write and then solve the equation to find the third angle.

_____

_____

2. Two angles in a triangle are 65° and 35°. Write and then solve the equation to find the third angle.

_____

_____

Find the missing angle measure in each figure.

3.

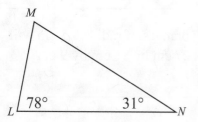

$m\angle M =$ _____

4.

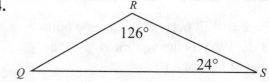

$m\angle Q =$ _____

Use the Triangle Sum Theorem to find the measure of each angle in degrees.

5.

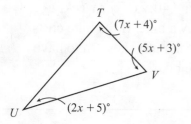

$m\angle T =$ _____

$m\angle U =$ _____

$m\angle V =$ _____

6.

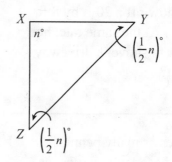

$m\angle X =$ _____

$m\angle Y =$ _____

$m\angle Z =$ _____

MIXED REVIEW

Write in exponent form.

7. $4 \times 4 \times 4 \times 4 \times 4$

8. $10 \times 10 \times 10$

9. $8 \times 8 \times 8$

10. $\frac{1}{4} \times \frac{1}{4} \times \frac{1}{4} \times \frac{1}{4}$

_____   _____   _____   _____

124

Exterior Angles

Use the Exterior Angles Theorem to find the measure of each angle in degrees.

1.

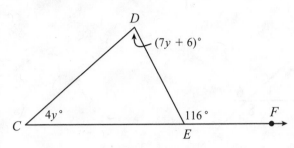

m∠C = _____

m∠D = _____

m∠DEC = _____

2.

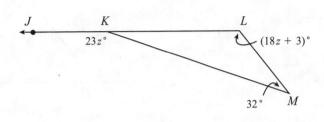

m∠L = _____

m∠MKL = _____

m∠MKJ = _____

3. What is the corresponding exterior angle for a 63° interior angle?

_____

4. If two interior angles of a triangle are 37° and 42°, what is the exterior angle of the third angle?

_____

5. What is the exterior angle for each angle of a square? a rectangle?

_____

6. What is the exterior angle for each angle of an equilateral triangle?

_____

Name _____   Date _____

Exploring Triangles

Use the figure for Exercises 1–11.

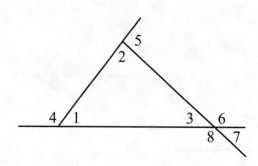

Tell which two angle measures have a sum equal to the measure of the given angle.

1. $\angle 4$ _____   **2.** $\angle 5$ _____   **3.** $\angle 8$ _____

Find each indicated angle measure.

4. $m\angle 3 = 40°$ and $m\angle 2 = 75°$. Find $m\angle 1$.   _____

5. $m\angle 1 = 50°$ and $m\angle 2 = 70°$. Find $m\angle 6$.   _____

6. $m\angle 1 = 45°$ and $m\angle 3 = 35°$. Find $m\angle 5$.   _____

7. $m\angle 2 = 74°$ and $m\angle 3 = 41°$. Find $m\angle 4$.   _____

8. $m\angle 4 = 135°$ and $m\angle 2 = 70°$. Find $m\angle 3$.   _____

9. $m\angle 8 = 143°$ and $m\angle 1 = 67°$. Find $m\angle 2$.   _____

10. $m\angle 5 = 118°$ and $m\angle 3 = 38°$. Find $m\angle 1$.   _____

11. In the triangle, $m\angle 1 = 62°$, $m\angle 2 = 78°$, and $m\angle 3 = 40°$. Find $m\angle 4 + m\angle 5 + m\angle 6$.

_____

WRITER'S CORNER

12. What generalization can you make about the sum of the measures of the exterior angles of a triangle?

_____

_____

126

Proving the Pythagorean Theorem

Use the Exterior Angles Theorem to find the measure of each angle in degrees.

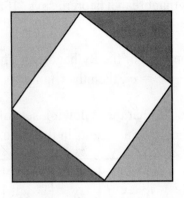

1. Draw a right triangle on a piece of paper and cut it out. Make one leg shorter than the other.

2. Trace your triangle onto another piece of paper four times, arranging the triangles as shown. For each triangle, label the shorter leg a, the longer leg b, and the hypotenuse c.

3. What is the area of the unshaded square?

_____

Label the unshaded square with its area.

4. Trace your original triangle onto a piece of paper four times again, arranging the triangles as shown. Draw a line outlining a larger square that is the same size as the figure you made in Exercise 2.

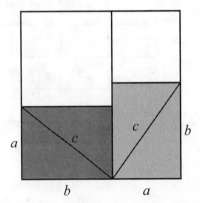

5. What is the area of the unshaded square at the top right of the figure in Exercise 4? at the top left?

_____

Label the unshaded squares with their areas.

6. What is the total area of the unshaded regions of the figure in Exercise 5?

_____

7. Tell whether the figures in Exercise 2 and Exercise 4 have the same area and explain why.

_____

8. Do the unshaded regions of the figures in Exercise 2 and Exercise 4 have the same area. Explain.

_____

_____

9. Write an equation relating the area of the unshaded region in Exercise 2 to the unshaded region in Exercise 4.

_____

The Converse of the Pythagorean Theorem

Decide whether the converse of the Pythagorean Theorem is true.

The Pythagorean Theorem says "If a triangle is a right triangle, then $a^2 + b^2 = c^2$."

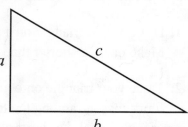

The converse of the Pythagorean Theorem says "If $a^2 + b^2 = c^2$, then the triangle is a right triangle."

1. Verify that the following sets of lengths make the equation $a^2 + b^2 = c^2$ true. Record your results in the table.

a	b	c	Is $a^2 + b^2 = c^2$ true?	Makes a right triangle?
3	4	5		
5	12	13		
7	24	25		
8	15	17		
20	21	29		

2. For each set of lengths in the table, cut strips of grid paper with a width of one square and lengths that correspond to the values of a, b, and c.

3. For each set of lengths, use the strips of grid paper to try to form a right triangle. An example using the first set of lengths is shown here. Record your findings in the table.

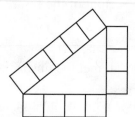

4. Based on your observations, explain whether you think the converse of the Pythagorean Theorem is true.

_____

_____

_____

Name _____ Date _____

Exploring Right Triangles

Name the hypotenuse and legs of each right triangle.

1. 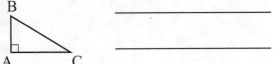 _____

_____

2.  _____

_____

3.  _____

_____

4. 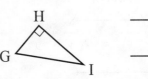 _____

_____

5. 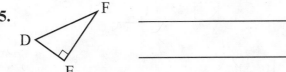 _____

_____

6. 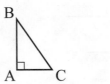 _____

_____

Decide whether the three sides form a right triangle. Write *yes* or *no*.

7. 12 cm, 17 cm, 20 cm _____

8. 3 in., 5 in., 4 in. _____

9. 13 ft, 5 ft, 12 ft _____

10. 7 yd, 3 yd, 9 yd _____

11. 30 cm, 16 cm, 34 cm _____

12. 3 in., 14 in., 6 in. _____

MIXED REVIEW

Find each value.

13. 6!

_____

14. 9!

_____

15. 12!

_____

16. $\frac{8!}{4!}$

_____

17. $\frac{10!}{5!}$

_____

Exploring the Pythagorean Theorem

Use a graph-paper diagram with squares to decide whether each triangle is a right triangle.

1. 6, 8, 10

2. 7, 10, 11

3. 12, 35, 37

_____   _____   _____

Use the Pythagorean Theorem to determine whether each triangle is a right triangle.

4. 4, 7, 8 _____

$4^2 +$ _____ $\overset{?}{=}$ _____

_____ $+$ _____ $\overset{?}{=}$ _____

_____ □ _____

5. 5, 12, 13 _____

_____ $+$ _____ $\overset{?}{=} 13^2$

_____ $+$ _____ $\overset{?}{=}$ _____

_____ □ _____

6. 5, 6, 9 _____

_____ $+ 6^2 \overset{?}{=}$ _____

_____ $+$ _____ $\overset{?}{=}$ _____

_____ □ _____

7. 12, 16, 20 _____

$12^2 +$ _____ $\overset{?}{=}$ _____

_____ $+$ _____ $\overset{?}{=}$ _____

_____ □ _____

8. 9, 12, 15

9. 4, 5, 6

10. 10, 24, 26

_____   _____   _____

NUMBER SENSE

---

11. The sum of the squares of the numbers 4 and 3 is 25. The ratio of the numbers is 4:3. Find two other pairs of numbers whose ratio is $\frac{4}{3}$.

_____

Determine the sum of the squares of those numbers. What is the relation between that sum and 25?

_____

Applying the Pythagorean Theorem

Find each missing measure. Round to the nearest tenth when necessary.

1.
8 in.
10 in.
?

2.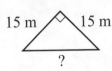
15 m   15 m
?

3.
12 m   ?
5 m

_____   _____   _____

4. $a = 6$ cm $b = 9$ cm

$c =$ _____

5. $a = 8$ in. $b = 15$ in.

$c =$ _____

Tell whether the three sides form a right triangle. Write *yes* or *no*.

6. 15 m, 15 m, 20 m

_____

7. 15 in., 36 in., 39 in.

_____

MIXED APPLICATIONS

8. Find the length of the guy wire supporting the antenna in the figure.

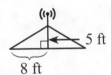
5 ft
8 ft

_____

9. Ted is making a red and yellow quilt with dimensions 72 in. by 90 in. How many sq ft of fabric does he need?

_____

10. Carol caught $1\frac{1}{2}$ times as many fish as Jorge. Together they caught 15 fish. How many did Jorge catch?

_____

EVERYDAY MATH CONNECTION

11. You want to fence a right triangular piece of land. The lengths of two shorter sides are 120 ft and 50 ft. What is the length of the third side?_____

How many feet of fencing are required to enclose the piece of land?   _____

The Pythagorean Theorem

Find the length of the missing side of each triangle.

1.
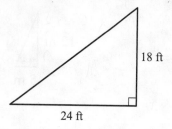
18 ft
24 ft

2.
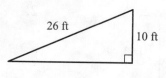
26 ft
10 ft

_____   _____

Find the missing length in each right triangle using $a^2 + b^2 = c^2$.

3. $a = 6$, $b = 8$, $c =$ _____

4. $a = 9$, $b =$ _____, $c = 15$

5. $a =$ _____, $b = 8$, $c = 17$

6. $a = 3$, $b =$ _____, $c = 5$

7. $a =$ _____, $b = 24$, $c = 25$

8. $a = 8$, $b = 15$, $c =$ _____

9. $a = 16$, $b = 12$, $c =$ _____

10. $a = 5$, $b =$ _____, $c = 13$

NUMBER SENSE

11. If you are given the length of the hypotenuse and one leg, does it matter whether you solve for a or b? Explain.

_____

_____

12. If the leg lengths of a right triangle are both whole numbers, will the hypotenuse always be a whole number? Explain.

_____

_____

132

Name _____ Date _____

Using the Pythagorean Theorem

Find each unknown length to the nearest tenth.

1.
3 m   a
4 m

2.
2 mm   6 mm
b

3.
5 m
2 m
a

4.
2 mm   c
1 mm

_____   _____   _____   _____

Solve. Round the solutions to the nearest tenth.

5.
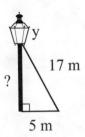
y
17 m
?
5 m

How high is the
lamppost?

6.
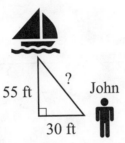
55 ft   ?   John
30 ft

How far is the boat
from John?

7.
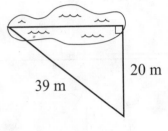
39 m   20 m

What is the length of
the pond?

_____   _____   _____

MIXED APPLICATIONS

8. John's kite is 45 ft above the ground.
A tree is directly under the kite. John is
standing 12 ft away from the tree. How
long is the kite string to the nearest tenth?

9. Meg is 4 years older than Steve, who is twice
as old as Pat. If Meg is 24, how old is Pat?

_____

_____

WRITER'S CORNER

10. Use the drawing to write a problem of your own. Solve.

28 ft
21 ft   ?

_____

Practice the Pythagorean Theorem

Find the length of the missing side in each figure. Approximate square roots of non-perfect squares to the nearest tenth without using a calculator.

1.

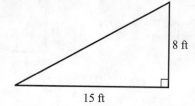

8 ft

15 ft

2.

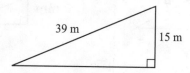

39 m   15 m

_____

3.

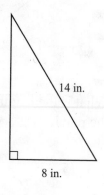

14 in.

8 in.

4.

8 cm

4 cm

_____

5. Find *s*, the diagonal of the bottom of the box. Leave the answer in radical form.

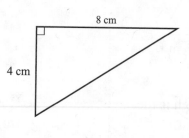

r   2 ft

s   1 ft

12 ft

_____

6. Find *r*, the diagonal of the box, to the nearest hundredth. Hint: Use the height of the box and the length of *s*.

_____

7. What is the longest flagpole (in whole feet) that could be shipped in a box that measures 1 ft by 2 ft by 12 ft?

_____

The Pythagorean Theorem in the Coordinate Plane

Approximate the length of the hypotenuse to the nearest tenth without using a calculator.

1.
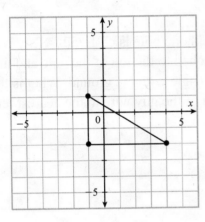

2.
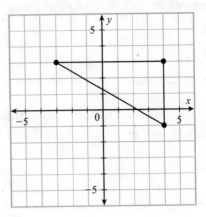

3.
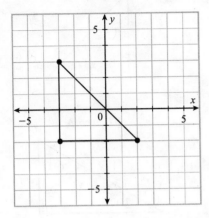

4.
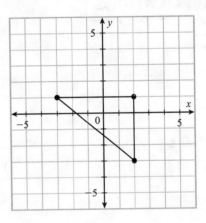

5. Estimate and then find the length of side $\overline{AB}$ of $\triangle ABC$ to the nearest thousandth.

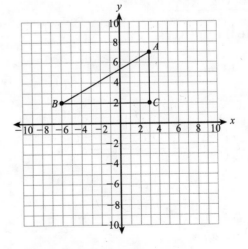

Core Skills Math, Grade 8

Name _____ Date _____

Exploring Special Right Triangles

Use Figure A to find each unknown length.
Write the answer in simplest radical form.

1. $a = 5$, $c =$ _____

2. $a = 7$, $c =$ _____

3. $c = 3$, $b =$ _____

4. $c = 12$, $a =$ _____

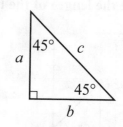

Figure A

Use Figure B to find each unknown length.
Write the answer in simplest radical form.

5. $c = 6$, $a =$ _____

6. $c = 4$, $b =$ _____

7. $c = 10$, $b =$ _____

8. $a = 9$, $c =$ _____

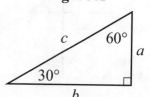

Figure B

MIXED APPLICATIONS

9. About how high is the kite?

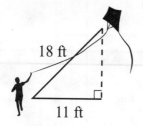

10. A telephone pole is 45 ft tall. A guy wire is attached to the top of the pole and makes a 45° angle with the ground. What is the length of the guy wire to the nearest tenth?

_____

_____

MIXED REVIEW

Compute the answers.

11. $4 + {-13} =$ _____

12. $-3 + {-11} =$ _____

13. $-17 + 5 =$ _____

14. $41 + {-5} =$ _____

15. $-30 - 12 =$ _____

16. $-7 - {-12} =$ _____

17. $8 - {-8} =$ _____

18. $-4 - {-4} =$ _____

136

Formula for Distance Between Two Points

Find the distance between each pair of points to the nearest tenth.

1. (5, 3) and (5, 7)

_____

2. (-4, 9) and (3, 9)

_____

3. (0, -8) and (0, -1)

_____

4. (3, 2) and (7, 5)

_____

5. (1, -3) and (6, 9)

_____

6. (-5, 11) and (4, -1)

_____

7. (0, 0) and (-6, 8)

_____

8. (0, -5) and (12, 0)

_____

9. (5, -4) and (1, -7)

_____

10. (-3, 4) and (5, -1)

_____

11. (-1, -2) and (-1, -9)

_____

12. (5, 5) and (6, 6)

_____

Answer Key

Page 1

1. closer to 5; 22 is closer to 25 than 16.
2. 4.6904158
3. 400
4. 1,024
5. 10.24
6. 9.1204
7. 13
8. 9
9. 25
10. 2.5
11. 0.25
12. 22
13. 2.2
14. 16
15. 1.6
16. 0.16
17. $2.50
18. 21.2
19. 46,000
20. 750,000
21. 70,000
22. 682,000
23. divide; 8
24. add; 14
25. subtract; 160
26. divide; 14
27. subtract; 272
28. multiply; 9

Page 2

1. 5.83
2. 9.06
3. 6.71
4. 10.20
5. 8.43
6. 4.36
7. 4.90
8. 6.40
9. 6.32
10. 4.58
11. 7.48
12. 6.24
13. 4.80
14. 6.86
15. 8.06
16. 5.92
17. 3.61
18. 8.89
19. 8.66
20. 9.85
21. 9.43
22. 5.48
23. 9.75
24. 3.46
25. 7.55

Page 3

1. SR
2. SR
3. S
4. N
5. SR
6. 9
7. 196
8. 49
9. 169
10. 256
11. 0.36
12. $\frac{16}{25}$
13. $\frac{25}{144}$
14. $\frac{169}{36}$
15. 11, −11
16. 16, −16
17. 14, −14
18. 20, −20
19. 30, −30
20. 7
21. 9
22. 12
23. 8
24. 15
25. 18 min
26. 120 m
27. 11

Page 4

1. 225
2. 8
3. 100
4. −5
5. $\frac{1}{16}$
6. 14
7. 4.4521
8. $-\frac{1}{11}$
9. $\frac{4}{81}$
10. 0.8
11. 64
12. 0.06
13. 4.9
14. 8.5
15. 12.1
16. 2.2
17. 10.0
18. 7.8
19. 17.3
20. 22.0
21. 4.6
22. 7.5
23. 3.6
24. 9.5
25. 10.5
26. 9.3
27. 15.8
28. 4.1
29. 400 ft
30. 11.2 cm
31. $252
32. 20.2 m
33. b.

Page 5

1. 9.4
2. 11.1
3. 4.5
4. 7.8
5. 1.73
6. 4.12
7. −5.83
8. 9.33
9. 11.14
10. 10.54
11. 0.20
12. −0.46
13. 2.2
14. 7
15. 3.3
16. 7.1
17. 5.5
18. No; The graph is not accurate enough.
19. Possible answers: Advantage: quick estimation of square roots. Disadvantage: does not give accurate values.

Page 6

1. 2^3
2. 5^4
3. 6^2
4. 4^4
5. 7^3
6. 14^2
7. 1^5
8. 10^3
9. 1.8^4
10. 128
11. 729
12. 49
13. 1
14. 4
15. 16
16. 2,401
17. 13
18. 25
19. 1
20. 1,296
21. 625
22. 9
23. 7
24. 16
25. 8
26. 4
27. 0
28. 1
29. 0
30. 3
31. 2
32. 9
33. 10
34. 5
35. 3
36. 1
37. 13
38. 32.768 cm^3
39. 9 days
40. 8.8
41. 1,200,000

Page 7

1. <
2. >
3. <
4. <
5. >
6. <
7. >
8. >
9. <
10. >
11. =
12. =
13. <
14. >
15. $-\sqrt{4}$, $\sqrt{4}$, $(\sqrt{4})^3$, 4^2,
16. $\sqrt{2}$, $\sqrt{4}$, $\sqrt{7}$, π, $\sqrt{25}$
17. $-\frac{1}{3}$, $\sqrt{7}$, π, $\sqrt{11}$
18. $\sqrt{7}$, $\sqrt{9}$, π, $\sqrt{16}$, 5
19. $\sqrt{4}$, $\sqrt{7}$, π, 3.5, 8
20. $\sqrt{2}$, $\sqrt{4}$, $\sqrt{8}$, π, $\sqrt{13}$
21. $-\sqrt{49}$, $\frac{1}{3}$, 4, $\sqrt{36}$
22. $\sqrt{\frac{7}{2}}$, 2, $\sqrt{7}$
23. π, $\sqrt{10}$, 3.5
24. 1.5, $\sqrt{3}$, $\sqrt{\frac{12}{3}}$
25. $\sqrt{24}$, $2\sqrt{7}$, 2π

Page 8

1. 1,000,000; 10,000,000
2. 0.0001; 0.00001
3. 3×3, 9; 3, 3; 1, 1
4. $\left(\frac{1}{3}\right)^2$, $\frac{1}{9}$; $\left(\frac{1}{3}\right)^3$, $\frac{1}{27}$; $\left(\frac{1}{3}\right)^4$, $\frac{1}{81}$
5. 10^{-5}
6. 3^{-9}
7. 10^{-11}
8. 6^{-3}
9. $\left(\frac{1}{10}\right)^9$
10. $\left(\frac{1}{2}\right)^{14}$
11. $\left(\frac{1}{4}\right)^8$
12. $\left(\frac{1}{10}\right)^{12}$
13. 10^{-5}
14. 10^{-7}
15. $x = 6$ cm
16. $x = 5$ mm
17. $0.32
18. $0.56
19. $2.19

Page 9

1. 5^{-1}
2. 10^{-7}
3. 8^{-3}
4. 10^{-2}
5. 2^{-5}
6. 2^{-6}
7. 3^{-3}
8. 10^{-6}
9. 5^{-2}
10. $\frac{1}{10,000}$ or 0.0001
11. $\frac{1}{10,000,000}$ or 0.0000001
12. $\frac{1}{1,000,000}$ or 0.000001
13. $\frac{1}{32}$ or 0.03125

14. $\frac{1}{3}$ or $0.\overline{3}$
15. $\frac{1}{10}$ or 0.1
16. $\frac{1}{81}$ or 0.01234568
17. $\frac{1}{125}$ or 0.008
18. $\frac{1}{81}$ or 0.01234568
19. $\frac{1}{100}$ or 0.01
20. $\frac{1}{16}$ or 0.0625
21. $\frac{1}{121}$ or 0.008264463
22. $-\frac{1}{6}$ or $-0.1\overline{6}$
23. $-\frac{1}{27}$ or $0.\overline{037}$
24. $\frac{1}{25}$ or 0.04
25. $\frac{1}{64}$ or 0.015625
26. $-\frac{1}{12}$ or $-0.08\overline{3}$
27. $\frac{1}{144}$ or $0.0069\overline{4}$
28. negative exponent
29. positive exponent
30. No; All the numbers are the quotient of 1 and a positive number; thus all the numbers are positive.

Page 10

1. $1 + 9$
2. $4 + -4$
3. $2 - (-3)$
4. $-9 - (-9)$
5. $-10 - 1$
6. $-7 - (-2)$
7. 2^{10}
8. 4^9
9. 8^{11}
10. 14^{-6}
11. 9^{-9}
12. 3^1 or 3
13. 7^{-8}
14. 6^{13}
15. $(-10)^5$
16. $(-5)^{-5}$
17. $(-6)^{-1}$
18. 4^1 or 4
19. 10^5
20. 12^1 or 12
21. 8^2
22. 9^9
23. 11^{-12}
24. 3^1
25. 10^3
26. 2^{-12}
27. $(-9)^9$
28. $(-7)^{-10}$
29. $(4.2)^{-1}$
30. 7^{25} bacteria

Page 11

1. 10^{-5}
2. 10^{-4}
3. 7.05
4. 2.119
5. 3.64×10^{-5}
6. 7.51×10^{-3}
7. 1.0005×10^{-1}
8. 1.094×10^{3}
9. 9.9×10^{-7}
10. 4.101×10^{-2}
11. 1.05×10^{4}
12. 8.9×10^{3}
13. 0.00074
14. 0.083
15. 0.00195
16. 0.000028
17. 5,450
18. 920,000
19. 0.0006091
20. 0.909
21. 300,000 km/sec
22. 6.048×10^{5} sec
23. 3.62×10^{-6}, 3.62×10^{-2}, 4.1×10^{-2}, 4.1×10^{7}, 4.1×10^{9}

Page 12

1. 500
2. 145,000
3. 6,072,000
4. 0.0048
5. 0.0000741
6: 0.00019
7. 300,000,000
8. 7,000,000,000
9. 266,450
10. 0.0057832
11. 0.000762953
12. 8,510,000,000,000
13. 4.1×10^{3}
14. 5.4×10^{-6}
15. 9.92×10^{6}
16. 8.0×10^{-3}
17. 7.05×10^{4}
18. 3.01×10^{-4}
19. $6.853429781 \times 10^{9}$
20. 1.35677×10^{5}
21. 8.8×10^{-4}
22. $1.246,912 \times 10^{6}$
23. 7.629×10^{-5}
24. 5.64372×10^{5}

Page 13

1. 1.2×10^{4}
2. 5.7×10^{10}
3. 4.3×10^{-4}
4. 8.76×10^{-9}
5. 2.4×10^{-3}
6. 1.7×10^{-7}
7. 9×10^{-6}
8. 8.045×10^{7}
9. 6.3×10^{9}
10. 6×10^{-7}
11. 400,000
12. 5,700
13. 9,000,000
14. 500
15. 33,000,000
16. 0.0009
17. 0.064
18. 2,300
19. 900,000
20. 0.0000005
21. 6.7×10^{-6}
22. Three hundred eighty-five million
23. 1.25×10^{7} grains; 9.2×10^{-4} in.

Page 14

1. 6.96×10^{8}
2. 7.28×10^{5}
3. 6.104×10^{8}
4. 5.586×10^{13}
5. 5.2843×10^{9}
6. 1.04×10^{6}
7. 2.52×10^{3}
8. 8.523×10^{13}
9. 6.3055×10^{7}
10. 4.9032×10^{8}
11. $4.37807701 \times 10^{12}$
12. 2.2999788×10^{8}
13. 4.54926×10^{15}
14. 1.65635×10^{6}
15. 4.877×10^{3}
16. 1.716×10^{11}
17. 5.32×10^{12}
18. 6.11×10^{14}
19. 1.924×10^{23}
20. 7.84×10^{29}
21. 1.8×10^{6}
22. 3.1×10^{3}
23. 6×10^{-2}
24. 1.2×10^{7}
25. 1.2204×10^{22}
26. 1.721096×10^{28}
27. 2×10^{7}
28. 1.73×10^{8}

Page 15

1. 4.94×10^{13} cells
2. 4.2875×10^{-5} cubic meters
3. 1.595×10^{13} ft^2
4. 1.298×10^{18} miles
5. 4.33×10^{7} people
6. about 7 people per square mile
7. 20.52; there are about 20 people in China for every 1 person in France.

Page 16

1. 5
2. 9
3. 2
4. 13
5. 6
6. 2
7. 6
8. 4
9. 11
10. 9
11. 15
12. 8
13. 3
14. 1
15. 16
16. 16
17. 10
18. 4
19. 1
20. 3
21. 7
22. 5
23. 11
24. 7
25. 8
26. 10
27. 12
28. 13
29. 15
30. 14
31. 14
32. 12
33. 47
34. 362
35. 26
36. 448
37. $2^{3} \times 3$
38. 2^{5}
39. $2^{2} \times 29$

140

Page 17

1. $m = 38$
2. $k = 77$
3. $z = 75$
4. $w = 84$
5. $g = 68$
6. $t = 11.4$
7. $s = 6.1$
8. $r = 29$
9–12. Variables will vary.
9. b = number of band instruments; $b - 10 = 47$
10. m = number of meters; $m - 25.6 = 84.3$
11. $r - 55 = 248$; $r = 303$; $303
12. $m - 4 = 11$; $m = 15$; $15 + x = 53$; $x = 38$; 38 years old
13. 58
14. 22
15. 4
16. 1
17. $x = 21$
18. $c = 47$
19. $y = 1.7$
20. $z = 0$

Page 18

1. $n = 8$
2. $x = 47$
3. $q = 52$
4. $r = 3$
5. $t = 15$
6. $s = 125$
7. $p = 10.4$
8. $b = 20$
9. $k = 4$
10. $m = 50$
11. $j = 0.6$
12. $y = 4$
13. $s = 123$
14. $a = 23.6$
15. $c = 25.8$
16. $k = 86$
17. $e = 32$
18. $h = 0.4$
19. $n = 5.375$
20. $t = 3$
21. $9x = 1{,}308.24$; $x = 145.36$; $145.36
22. $(\$450 - \$150) \div 30$; $10 per hour
23. 0.125 cm^3

Page 19

1. multiplication
2. division
3. subtraction
4. addition
5. $w = 24$
6. $n = 63$
7. $x = 170$
8. $b = 216$
9. $y = 2.32$
10. $k = 25.2$
11. $d = 148$
12. $c = 68$
13. $n = 10.34$
14. $a = 172$
15. $y = 49$
16. $h = 744$
17. $\frac{n}{5} = 15.5$; $n = 77.5$; $77.50
18. $30n = 120$; $n = 4$; 4 persons
19. $x = 13$
20. $y = 72$
21. $b = 4.7$
22. $x = 8$
23. $k = 7.2$
24. $p = 55$
25. $l = 44$
26. $m = 95$

Page 20

1. $a = -6$
2. $b = 5$
3. $c = 16$
4. $d = 14.3$
5. $e = 2$
6. $f = -5.5$
7. $g = 0.9$
8. $h = -9$
9. $j = 49$
10. $k = 4.3$
11. $m = -2.99$
12. $n = -9$
13–15. Variables will vary.
13. $x + 1.3 = 3.2$
14. $y - 6.3 = -6.3$
15. $\frac{4}{5}c = 32$; $c = 40$; 40 cars
16. 12.7 inches
17. 36
18. 15%
19. 80
20. 43.2
21. 2.88
22. 40%

Page 21

1. subtraction; multiplication
2. addition; division
3. addition; multiplication
4. subtraction; division
5. $x = 25$
6. $d = 162$
7. $w = 4$
8. $c = 3$
9. $b = 4$
10. $a = 3$
11. $t = 24$
12. $k = 3$
13. $11c - 7 = 70$
14. $\frac{n}{8} + 4 = 28$
15. $2w - 10 = 35$; $w = 22.5$; 22.5 ft
16. $0.0625 + 0.625 \times 2.4$
17. $t + 3t + 8t = 180$; $15°$, $45°$, $120°$

Page 22

1. $a = -2$
2. $b = 2$
3. $c = 29$
4. $t = -0.5$
5. $h = -2$
6. $y = 1$
7. $j = -2$
8. $k = 0.7$
9. $w = -2$
10. $m = -45$
11. $n = 28$
12. $r = -9$
13–15. Key sequences may vary.
13. $6 - 5 = \times 4 \div 3$
14. $6 + 3 = \times 3 \div 2$
15. $2.1 - 3 = \times 7 \div 3$
16. $2x - 3 = 15$; $x = 9$; 9 goals
17. $12 + 4.5(12) = x$; 66 dolls
18. a

Page 23

1. $n = 21$
2. $q = 13$
3. $a = -1$
4. $w = 20\frac{1}{10}$ or $\frac{201}{10}$
5. $x = 8$
6. $b = \frac{5}{9}$
7. $t = 1\frac{19}{21}$ or $\frac{40}{21}$
8. $t = 1\frac{1}{2}$ or $\frac{3}{2}$
9. $z = 51\frac{1}{2}$ or $\frac{103}{2}$
10. $r = 8\frac{7}{18}$ or $\frac{151}{18}$

141

11. $h = 5\frac{1}{8}$ or $\frac{41}{8}$

12. $k = 37\frac{1}{2}$ or $\frac{75}{2}$

13. $9.60

14. Divide by 2 or multiply by $\frac{1}{2}$;
$\frac{5}{8}, \frac{5}{16}, \frac{5}{32}$

15. $<$

16. $=$

17. $>$

18. $=$

19. $1\frac{7}{12}$ or $\frac{19}{12}$

20. $\frac{7}{30}$

21. $3\frac{2}{15}$

22. $2\frac{2}{5}$

Page 24

1. $x = 5$
2. $x = 3$
3. $x = 2$
4. $x = -4$
5. $x = 3$
6. $x = 5$
7. $x = 2$
8. $x = -2$
9. $x = 16$
10. $x = 2.5$ or $2\frac{1}{2}$
11. $x = 3.12$
12. $x = 1$
13. $x = 22$
14. $x = \frac{1}{4}$ or 0.25
15. $x = 2\frac{1}{2}$ or 2.5
16. $x = 2\frac{15}{49}$ or 2.3
17. $x = 1$
18. $x = \frac{47}{160}$ or 0.29

Page 25

1. 3 lessons
2. 1 lesson
3. 2 lessons
4. Amanda is 22; her father is 44.
5. 39
6. $21.00
7. 17

Page 26

1. $x = 8$, true
2. $-5 = -5$ or $0 = 0$, true
3. $0 = -7$ or $2 = -5$, false
4. one solution
5. infinitely many solutions
6. Accept any answer other than 1.
7. 4

Page 27

1–6. Variables will vary.

1. $x + 587.46 = 675$; $x = 87.54$; $87.54
2. $3s = 225$; $s = 75$; $75
3. $l + 4.7 = 7$; $l = 2.3$; 2.3 T more
4. $p - 76 = 1897$; $p = 1973$; 1973
5. $4k = 2.4$; $k = 0.6$; 0.6 gal
6. $\frac{d}{12} = 12.50$; $d = 150$; $150
7. 7 quarters and 3 dimes
8. no
9. $1,245
10. 79 cameras

Page 28

1–2. Check drawings.

3. slide
4. flip
5. turn
6. slide
7. two turns
8. 113 tiles
9. turn
10. slide
11. flip
12. turn

Page 29

1–2. Check drawings.

3. slide
4. turn
5. flip
6. acute angle
7. Check drawings.
8. slide
9. Answers will vary.

Page 30

1. true
2. false
3. true
4. true
5. false
6. true
7–8. Check drawings
9. 25%
10. $\frac{5}{9}$ or 5:9
11. Possible answers: mirror, water, glass.

Page 31

1. (3, 2)
2. (-1, 8)
3. (3, 4)

4. (3, -6)
5. (5, -2)
6. (2, 0)
7. (-4, -5)
8. (-4, 1)
9. (3, 5)
10. (2, -8)
11–13.

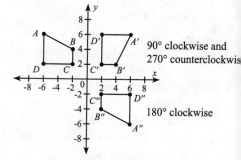

90° clockwise and
270° counterclockwise

180° clockwise

14. $A'(5, -7)$, $B'(5, -2)$, $C'(1, -4)$, $D'(1, -6)$
15. 10:30 A.M.
16. Check drawing.

Page 32

1–4. Check Drawings

5. 53.29 in.²
6. 84 cm²
7. 28.26 in.²
8. 7.28 mm²

Page 33

1. (2, -2), (2, -4), (-3, -4), (-3, -2)
2. (4, -3), (4, -1), (-1, -1), (-1, -3)
3. (-2, 2), (-2, 4), (3, 4), (3, 2)
4. (-2, -2), (-2, -4), (3, -4), (3, -2)
5. (-1, 3), (-1, 5), (-6, 5), (-6, 3)
6. $5,200
7. $4,625
8. no mode

Page 34

1–3. Check work.

4. The translation does not change the length of the line segment.
5. The translation does not change the angle measures.
6. The translation does not change the orientation of segments such as parallel lines.
7. Translations preserve the shape and size of a figure.

Page 35

1–3. Check work.
4. The reflection does not change the length of the line segments.
5. The reflection does not change the angle measures.
6. The reflection does not change parallel lines.
7. Reflections preserve the shape and size of a figure.
8. The rotation maps line segments to line segments of equal length and angles to angles with equal measure. Rotations preserve the shape and size of a figure.

Page 36

1–5. Check drawings.
6. They have the same size and shape, just a different orientation.
7. translation, rotation
8. =
9. <
10. =

Page 37

1. Possible answer: $(x, y) \rightarrow$ $(-x, y)$ and $(x, y) \rightarrow (x - 1, y)$
2. Possible answer: $(x, y) \rightarrow$ $(x + 1, y)$ and $(x, y) \rightarrow (-x, y)$
3. 90°
4. Translate the rotated figure up 2 units and right 1 unit.
5. 90°
6. (2, 4), (4, 4), (4, 1), (2, 1)
7. Translate the rotated figure down 6 units.
8. There is no sequence of translations, reflections, and/or rotations that can transform one figure into the other. The figures are not the same size.

Page 38

1. Order may vary:
   (2, -1), (1, -1), (1, -2), (-2, -2), (-2, 1), (-1, 1), (-1, 2)
2. 3
3. Order may vary:
   (6, -3), (3, -3), (3, -6), (-6, -6), (-6, 3), (-3, 3), (-3, 6)
4. Check drawings.

5. Each line segment in the image is three times longer than the corresponding line segment in the preimage.
6. The dilation does not change the angle measures.

Page 39

1. Order may vary:
   (4, 2), (0, 5), (-4, 2), (-2, 2), (-2, -4), (2, -4), (2, 2)
2. $\frac{1}{2}$
3. Order may vary:
   (2, 1), (0, 2.5), (-2, 1), (-1, 1), (-1, -2), (1, -2), (1, 1)
4. Check drawings.
5. Each line segment in the image is changed by the scale factor from the corresponding line segment in the preimage.
6. There would be no change. The image would be the same size and shape as the preimage.

Page 40

1. Order may vary:
   Preimage (0, 2), (0, -2), (-2, 0);
   Image (0, 3), (0, -3), (-3, 0)
2–3. Check drawings.
4. $\frac{1}{4}$
5. $\frac{1}{2}$

Page 41

1–5. Check drawings.
6. Order may vary: (3, 6), (3, -6), (-3, -6), (-3, 6)
7. same shape; rectangle 5 is three times the size of the original; same angle measures

Page 42

1. dilation by scale factor 2 with center at origin and $(x, y) \rightarrow$ $(x + 4, y + 6)$
2. If you translate the figure first, the center of the dilation will not be at the origin.
3. They are not congruent. They are similar.
4–5. Answers may vary.
4. dilation by scale factor $\frac{1}{2}$, translation up 5 units, reflection across y-axis

5. rotation of 180° about the origin, dilation by scale factor $\frac{1}{2}$, translation up 5 units.
6.

Page 43

1. a
2. c
3. b
4–7. Estimates may vary.
4. 1
5. $\frac{1}{2}$
6. 20
7. 8
8. about 5 oz
9. No; an estimate of the difference is 1 and $\frac{13}{5}$ more than 2.
10. about $2\frac{1}{2}$; about $2.50 higher

Page 44

1. $\frac{1}{3}$
2. $\frac{1}{8}$
3. $2\frac{7}{9}$ or $\frac{25}{9}$
4. $-\frac{3}{5}$
5. $-\frac{1}{4}$
6. $-6\frac{4}{7}$
7. -6.2
8. -0.6
9. -11.33
10. $\frac{5}{12}$
11. $-\frac{5}{14}$
12. $1\frac{11}{104}$ or $\frac{115}{104}$
13. $\frac{1}{5}$
14. $\frac{5}{22}$
15. $-\frac{7}{18}$
16. 4.2
17. 8.75
18. 5.19
19. 4.79
20. -6.79
21. -30.69
22. $5\frac{1}{4}$ dozen eggs or 63 eggs
23. 32.9°C
24. less than the original number

143

Page 45

1–17. Estimate may vary. Possible estimates are given.

1. $\frac{1}{2}$
2. 1
3. 6
4. 12
5. 36
6. 20
7. 32
8. 10
9. 72
10. 4
11. 6
12. 64; close estimate
13. 30; underestimate
14. 1; overestimate
15. 10; close estimate
16. 50; overestimate
17. 64; close estimate
18. about 45 acres
19. about $50
20. Possible estimates are: 1 c; 1 tsp; $\frac{1}{4}$ c; $\frac{1}{2}$ tbsp

Page 46

1. greater than 1
2. less than 1
3. less than 1
4. greater than 1
5. less than 1
6. greater than 1
7. greater than 1
8. less than 1
9. less than 1
10. greater than 1
11. greater than 1
12. less than 1

13–21. Estimates may vary.

13. 3
14. 2
15. $\frac{1}{2}$
16. 1
17. 8
18. $\frac{1}{2}$
19. 4
20. $\frac{1}{3}$
21. $\frac{1}{5}$
22. about 20 plants
23. about 8 lb
24. $\frac{1}{8}$

Page 47

1. $-\frac{1}{18}$
2. $\frac{3}{25}$
3. $-\frac{4}{21}$
4. $-\frac{16}{39}$
5. -1
6. $-\frac{1}{2}$
7. $\frac{5}{16}$
8. $-\frac{35}{72}$
9. -1.08
10. -13.68
11. 1
12. 20
13. -4
14. -17.1
15. -0.624
16. $-\frac{8}{15}$
17. -25
18. -1
19. -1.68
20. 9.3
21. 6.2
22. 3
23. -3.15
24. -0.3
25. 8
26. 0.4
27. 2
28. 14.78 inches
29. 27 years
30. Check problem.

Page 48

1. 0.75
2. 0.7
3. 0.35
4. 0.28125
5. 0.14
6. 0.4
7. 0.3125
8. 0.26
9. 0.625
10. 1.75
11. 0.12
12. 0.85
13. 0.4375
14. $0.\overline{27}$
15. $0.3\overline{8}$
16. $2.\overline{5}$
17. 0.075
18. 3.125
19. $0.3\overline{6}$
20. $0.1\overline{3}$
21. <
22. >
23. =
24. >
25. >
26. =
27. >
28. <
29. 4.875 pages
30. $2.6, 2.\overline{6}$; freestyle event
31. If the prime factors of the denominator of the fraction include only 2s and 5s, the fraction will terminate.

Page 49

1. $\frac{4}{5}$
2. $\frac{3}{25}$
3. $\frac{7}{10}$
4. $\frac{1}{20}$
5. $\frac{3}{40}$
6. $\frac{9}{20}$
7. $\frac{1}{4}$
8. $\frac{1}{50}$
9. $4\frac{1}{2}$
10. $3\frac{47}{50}$
11. $5\frac{6}{25}$
12. $8\frac{9}{25}$
13. $\frac{1}{10}$
14. $\frac{11}{20}$
15. $\frac{13}{100}$
16. $1\frac{1}{10}$
17. $3\frac{2}{5}$
18. $\frac{41}{50}$
19. $\frac{27}{100}$
20. $1\frac{4}{5}$
21. $0.3, \frac{1}{3}, \frac{2}{5}$
22. $\frac{3}{4}, \frac{5}{6}, \frac{7}{8}, 0.\overline{8}$
23. $0.4, \frac{1}{2}, \frac{6}{11}, 0.\overline{5}$
24. $\frac{1}{4}, \frac{1}{3}, 0.38, 0.45$
25. $1.2, 1.\overline{2}, 1\frac{1}{4}, 1\frac{2}{7}$
26. $0.\overline{1}, \frac{3}{25}, 0.125, \frac{2}{9}$
27. $\frac{7}{20}$ lb
28. Bertha
29. Answers will vary. Possible answer: 0.202002000…

144

Page 50

1. -13 m
2. $9.50
3. -7.7°F
4. 7°F per hour
5. 135 gal
6. Brand B
7. Check problem.

Page 51

1–2.

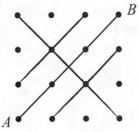

3. parallel, congruent
4. perpendicular, congruent
5. perpendicular, not congruent
6. neither, not congruent

7–8.

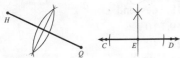

9. $\overline{PY}$
10. parallel
11. 5 bisectors

Page 52

1. c
2. a, d
3. e, h
4. b, f, g
5. $\overleftrightarrow{WX}, \overleftrightarrow{WY}, \overleftrightarrow{XY}$
6. $\overline{YX}, \overline{YW}, \overline{XW}$
7. true
8. true
9. true
10. true
11–12. Check drawings.
11. No; a segment is named by its endpoints.
12. $\angle JKL, \angle LKJ, \angle K$
13. line: 2 points; plane: 3 points

Page 53

1. Possible answer: $\angle 1$ and $\angle 5$
2. Possible answer: $\angle 2$ and $\angle 7$
3. alternate interior angles
4. same-side interior angles

5. congruent
6. supplementary
7. congruent
8. supplementary
9. congruent
10. congruent
11. true
12. false
13. false
14. true
15. $9\frac{1}{6}$
16. -5.198
17. 21.773
18. $2\frac{9}{16}$

Page 54

1. 150°
2. 150°
3. 150°
4. 100°
5. 100°
6. 80°
7. true
8. false
9. true
10. false
11. false
12. true
13. 16.7637
14. $\frac{6}{23}$
15. 150.2715
16. $8\frac{1}{100}$

Page 55

1. 70°
2. 110°
3. 70°
4. 110°
5. 70°
6. 70°
7. parallel
8. perpendicular
9. parallel
10. perpendicular
11. $\angle 5$
12. $\angle 6$
13. $\angle 7$
14. $\angle 8$
15. $\angle 1$ and $\angle 3$, $\angle 2$ and $\angle 4$, $\angle 5$ and $\angle 7$, $\angle 6$ and $\angle 8$
16. $\angle 6$
17. $\angle 5$
18. $\angle 7$
19. $\angle 8$

20. no
21. yes

Page 56

1–5. Check constructions.
6. 54 in.
7. $m\angle DEG = 86°$
8. Stu did not open the compass more than $\frac{1}{2}$ the length of the segment.

Page 57

1–3. Check constructions.
4. $m\angle E = 120°$, $DE = 6$ cm
5. $m\angle C = 70°$, $m\angle B = 80°$
6. $\triangle PAB \approx \triangle PDC$ by SAS. Thus, $AB = CD$. Mika measures the distance CD on land. This distance will be equal to distance AB.
7. Yes; since $\overrightarrow{SQ}$ bisects $\angle PSR$, $\angle PSQ \approx \angle RSQ$. $\overrightarrow{SR} \approx \overrightarrow{SQ}$ and $\overrightarrow{PS} \approx \overrightarrow{RS}$. Thus the triangles are congruent by SAS.

Page 58

1. $\frac{24}{32} = \frac{3}{4}$
2. $\frac{3}{8} = \frac{69}{184}$
3. $\frac{280}{444} = \frac{70}{111}$
4. $n = 210$
5. $13n = 60$
6. $25n = 32$
7. $100n = 200$
8. $n = 15$
9. $n = 17$
10. $n = 18$
11. $n = 16$
12. $n = 28$
13. $n = 56$
14. $n = 72$
15. $n = 252$
16. $n = 200$
17. $n = 105$
18. $n = 70$
19. $n = 25$
20. $n = 0.18$
21. $n = 2.55$
22. $n = 9.8$
23. $n = 1.96$
24. 12 football fans
25. 21 gal
26. 22 teeth

145

Page 59

1. $33\frac{1}{3}\%$
2. 75%
3. 80%
4. 15%
5. $33\frac{1}{3}\%$
6. 75%
7. $66\frac{2}{3}\%$
8. 25%
9. 25%
10. 125%
11. $12\frac{1}{2}\%$
12. 30%
13. $37\frac{1}{2}\%$
14. $46\frac{2}{3}\%$
15. 50%
16. 200%
17. 20%
18. 40%
19. 320%
20. 25%
21. 66 2/3%
22. 3/8
23. Check problem.

Page 60

1. c
2. a
3. b

4–15. Answers may vary.
4. $\frac{1}{3}$
5. $\frac{3}{4}$ or $\frac{4}{5}$
6. $\frac{2}{3}$
7. $\frac{9}{10}$ or $\frac{8}{9}$
8. about 25%
9. about 50%
10. about 75%
11. about $66\frac{2}{3}\%$
12. about 50%
13. about 280
14. about 1,600
15. about $33\frac{1}{3}\%$
16. 112 seeds
17. +, −

Page 61

1–8. Estimates may vary.
1. about $3.00
2. about $3.75
3. about $0.90
4. about $1.80
5. about $4.50
6. about $4.50
7. about $3.00
8. about $1.50
9. about $10.50
10. about $40
11. I = $3,840; A = $11,840
12. 3 paces
13. about 12,000 square miles

Page 62

1. Commutative Property of Addition
2. Distributive Property
3. Associative Property of Multiplication
4. Identity Property (Property of 0)
5. Commutative Property of Multiplication
6. Identity Property (Property of 1)
7. Distributive Property
8. 0
9. 1
10. 25, 60, 77
11. $(4 \times 0.90) + (4 \times 0.15) = 4 \times (0.90 + 0.15) = 4 \times 1.05 = 4.20;$ $4.20
12. $(21 + 9) + 47 = 30 + 47 = 77$
13. <
14. >
15. 15.0
16. 134.7

Page 63

1. Commutative Property of Addition
2. Identity Property (Property of 0)
3. Associative Property of Multiplication
4. Identity Property (Property of 1)
5. Additive Inverse Property
6. Distributive Property
7. -4
8. 238
9. 2
10. 33
11. -10
12. 422
13. 7
14. -160

15. 68 m
16. 22 lines
17. 27 mi

Page 64

1. $\frac{5}{10}$ or $\frac{1}{2}$
2. $-\frac{7}{3}$
3. $\frac{4}{1}$
4. $\frac{26}{10}$ or $\frac{13}{5}$
5. $\frac{8}{10}$ or $\frac{4}{5}$
6. $-\frac{15}{4}$
7. $\frac{225}{100}$ or $\frac{9}{4}$
8. $\frac{9}{5}$
9. >
10. <
11. <
12. <
13. $-2, -1\frac{2}{3}, \frac{1}{4}$
14. $\frac{4}{7}, \frac{3}{4}, 1\frac{2}{3}, 2, 2.3$
15. $-1\frac{1}{3}, -1.3, \frac{2}{5}, \frac{3}{6}, \frac{2}{3}$
16. $1, 1\frac{2}{5}, 1.45, 2\frac{3}{8}, 2.7$
17. 8:00 A.M.
18. descend
19. 10°C
20. 40°C
21. -17.8°C or $17\frac{7}{9}$°C

Page 65

2. Real, Rational, Whole, Integer
3. Real, Rational
4. Real, Irrational
5. Real, Irrational
6. Real, Rational, Integer
7. Real, Rational
8. Real, Rational
9. Real, Rational
10. $-10, -9.1, -\sqrt{13}, (0.39)^2, 3.14159..., 6\frac{1}{3}, 7.21212..., 210, 312$
11. 7; real, rational, whole, integer
12. 3.74..., real, irrational
13. 0.42..., real, irrational
14. 0.9; real, rational
15. 7, 63, 28

146

© Houghton Mifflin Harcourt Publishing Company

Answer Key, Core Skills Math, Grade 8

Page 66

1. 11
2. 15
3. 80
4. 52
5. 24
6. 21
7. 0
8. 90
9. 39
10. 32
11. 13
12. 6
13. 4
14. 4
15. 5
16. 2
17. 4
18. 2
19. 6
20. 11
21. 16
22. 16
23. 3
24. 6

Page 67

1–2.

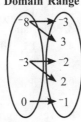

3. Exercise 1
4. Yes; Each element of the domain is matched to exactly one element of the range.
5. No: 5 is matched to more than one element of the range.
6. No; 16 and 9 are each matched to more than one element of the range.
7. Yes; Each element of the domain is matched to exactly one element of the range.
8. 8 units^2

Page 68

1. yes

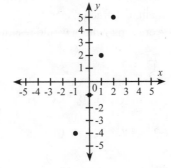

2. no

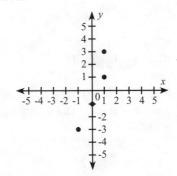

3. yes

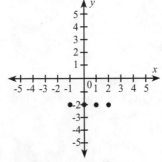

4. Solutions will vary. $y = 3x - 2$; (0, -2), (1, 1) (2, 4); yes
5. 240%
6. n^2

Page 69

1. (-4, -4), (1, 1), (3, 3), (-2, -2); yes
2. (-3, 2), (1, -4), (4, 1), (4, -2); no
3. Multiply each hour value by $10.
4. Subtract $5 from each original price.
5.

Growth of Plant					
Years, x	1	2	3	4	5
Height, y	28 in.	32 in.	36 in.	40 in.	44 in.

6. 3 hr
7. Check problem.

Page 70

1. 2 and 3

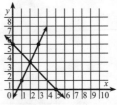

2. Length = 9 and width = 2

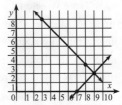

3. Length = 6 and width = 3

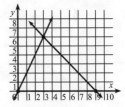

4. 3 and 7

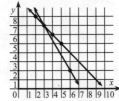

5. 8 pounds of pretzels and 4 pounds of cereal

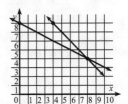

Page 71

1. A steep upward slope shows that attendance rose quickly.
2. The increase might coincide with summer break from school.
3. Segments 4 and 5; decrease might coincide with the end of summer vacation when school starts back.
4. The positive slope in segments 2 and 3 shows that the number of visitors increases as time passes. The negative slope in segments 4 and 5 shows that the number of visitors decreases as time passes.

147

Page 72

1.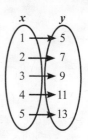

Number of Students (y-axis)
Time (weeks) (x-axis) 0 1 2 3 4 5

2. Possible answer: More students might come to tutoring right before the test. After the test, the number of students might decrease.

3.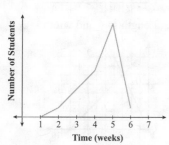

Number of Students (y-axis)
Time (weeks) (x-axis) 1 2 3 4 5 6 7

4. Possible answer: More students might come to tutoring each week.

5. Possible answer: The graph would shift upward before students would participate. Overall, trends would stay the same.

Page 73

1. Slowest growth: Phase 1; the curve is increasing, but not very steep. Fastest growth: Phase 2; the curve is increasing and steeper than Phase 1.

2. The graph is almost horizontal. The population is stable (not increasing or decreasing).

3. The graph is decreasing, so the number of microbes is decreasing.

4. The population is decreasing at first but begins to increase again.

5.

Fox Population

Population (y-axis)
Time (x-axis) t

6. The graph would show a steep decline at the point that represents the fire. Then as the forest grows again, the gradual increasing and decreasing pattern would resume.

Page 74

1–3. Answers may vary.
1. (-2, 3), (-1, 4), (0, 5), (1, 6)
2. (-2, -5), (-1, -4), (0, -3), (1, -2)
3. (-2, -4), (-1, -2), (0, 0), (1, 2)
4. no
5. no
6. yes
7. no
8. $y = 2 - x$; (-1, 3), ($-\frac{1}{2}$, $2\frac{1}{2}$), (0, 2), ($\frac{1}{2}$, $1\frac{1}{2}$), (1, 1)
9. $y = 10 - 4x$; (-1, 14), ($-\frac{1}{2}$, 12), (0, 10), ($\frac{1}{2}$, 8), (1, 6)
10. $y = 10 - x$; (-1, 11), ($-\frac{1}{2}$, $10\frac{1}{2}$), (0, 10), ($\frac{1}{2}$, $9\frac{1}{2}$), (1, 9)
11. $y = x + 3$
12. 1.5 hr listening; 3 hr reading
13. 64 km

Page 75

1. (2, 4)
2. (-6, -4)
3. $x = 0$
4. One solution is (4, 6).
5–8. Check graphs. Possible ordered pairs are given.
5. (-1, -3), (0, -2), (2, 0)
6. (-2, -3), (0, 1), (2, 5)
7. (-5, 0), (0, 5), (2, 7)
8. (-2, -6), (0, 0), (1, 3)
9. $y = 2x$; Check graph.
10. 8 hr
11. an infinite number

Page 76

1. a, c
2. c
3. a, c
4. b, c
5. a, c
6. a, b, c
7. c
8. a
9. b, c
10. a, b, c
11. a

12.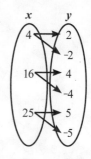

13.

x y
4   2
      -2
16   4
      -4
25   5
      -5

Page 77

1. 4, positive
2. -3, negative
3. 1, positive
4. $\frac{3}{7}$, positive
5. -5, negative
6. $\frac{2}{5}$, positive

Page 78

1. 15
2. 15; 15
3. constant
4. 36, 13, -10
5. variable
6. 15
7. 15
8. Yes; the graph appears to be a straight line through the origin.
9. 15
10. They are the same.
11. 15
12. =, =

Page 79

1. $-\frac{2}{3}$
2. $-\frac{2}{3}$
3. $-\frac{2}{3}$
4. the steepness of the line or the ratio of change in y to change in x
5. No; a line has a constant steepness (a constant rate of change), so the rate of change over any interval is the same.

Page 80

1. positive
2. slope = 200
3. Yes; the situation is a proportional relationship.
4. rate of change = $\frac{1}{3}$, slope = $\frac{1}{3}$
5. rate of change = 5, slope = 5
6. rate of change = 0.4, slope = 0.4

Page 81

1. $\frac{1}{1}$ or 1
2. $\frac{4}{3}$
3. $\frac{1}{2}$
4. $-\frac{3}{2}$
5. $-\frac{1}{2}$
6. $-\frac{3}{1}$ or -3
7. 0
8. $\frac{3}{1}$ or 3
9. $\frac{2}{7}$
10. negative
11. negative
12. positive
13. negative
14. positive
15. positive
16. $\frac{14}{51}$

Page 82

1. $\frac{4}{5}$
2. -3
3. $\frac{5}{3}$
4. $\frac{1}{8}$
5. 1
6. $\frac{3}{5}$
7. 0
8. 0
9. $\frac{5}{6}$
10. $\frac{2}{5}$
11. $y = 10x + 200$, slope 10
12. $y = 10x + 400$, slope 10
13. The commissions, which are dependent upon unit sales, are the same in each situation.

Page 83

1–6. Check drawings.
1. 20, 26; linear
2. -4, -3, -2, -1, 0; linear
3. 8, 17, 32, 53, 80; not linear
4. 17, 19, 21, 23, 25; linear
5. 9, 7, 5, 3, 1; linear
6. 1, 1, -7, -23; not linear

Page 84

1. 3, 4.5, 6, 7.5
2.

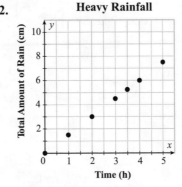

Heavy Rainfall

3. 5.25 cm
4. Check graph.
5. All of the points lie along a straight line.
6. $y = 50x + 100$
7. 400, 500, 600, 700, 800
8.

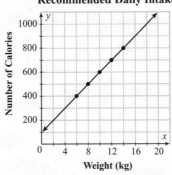

Recommended Daily Intake

9. the graph of the solutions is a straight line.

Page 85

1. Yes; the equation can be written in the form $y = mx + b$, and the graph of the solutions is a straight line.
2. No; the equation cannot be written in the form of $y = mx + b$, and the graph of the solutions is not a straight line.
3. Yes; the equation can be written in the form $y = mx + b$, and the graph of the solutions is a straight line.
4. Yes; the equation can be written in the form $y = mx + b$, and the graph of the solutions is a straight line.
5. No; the equation cannot be written in the form of $y = mx + b$, and the graph of the solutions is not a straight line.

6. Yes; the equation can be written in the form $y = mx + b$, and the graph of the solutions is a straight line.
7. (-1, -2) and (-2, -4) are not solutions of the equation. The correct solutions all lie on a line, so the equation is a linear equation.
8. Disagree; the equation can be written in the form of $y = mx + b$ where m is 0 and the graph of the solutions is a horizontal line.

Page 86

1. $(0, b)$; The value of x is 0 at the y-intercept.
2. $y - b$ or $b - y$
3. $x - 0$ or $0 - x$
4. b, x
5. $y = mx + b$
6. The y-intercept is 0, so the equation is $y = mx$.
7. $y = -4x + 6$
8. $y = \frac{5}{2}x - 3$

Page 87

1–7. Check graphs.
1. -2, -2, 5; 5; 2, 1
2.
3.
4. $-\frac{7}{4}$, 6
5. $\frac{7}{8}$, -4
6. -2, 12
7. $-\frac{5}{8}$, 5

149

Page 88

1. -0.004
2. $b = 59$
3. $y = -0.004x + 59$
4. $y = -0.004(5000) + 59 = 39°F$
5. $m = 0.0625$; the diver ascends at a rate of 0.0625 m/s.
6. -5; the diver starts 5 meters below the water's surface.
7. $y = 0.0625x - 5$
8. $m = \frac{180}{100}$ or $\frac{9}{5}$; $b = 32$; $y = \frac{9}{5}x + 32$ where $y = °F$ and $x = °C$
9. 98.6°F

Page 89

1. Table: -2; Graph: $-\frac{2}{3}$
2. The function in the table has a steeper graph because the absolute value of its slope is greater.
3. Table: $y = -2x - 1$; Graph: $y = -\frac{2}{3}x + 1$
4. the function represented on the graph
5. Table: -3; Graph: $\frac{1}{3}$
6. Table: -5; Graph: $\frac{7}{3}$

Page 90

1. $(1, -1)$

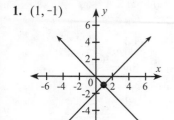

2. $(1, 5)$

3. $(-1, -4)$

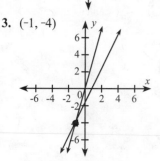

4. $x + y = 15$; $y = x + 3$; Mark: 9 hr; John 6 hr
5. $x + y = 18$; $y = 2x$; Jogging: 12 hr; Sit-ups: 6 hr
6. $\frac{10}{2}$ or 5
7. $\frac{13}{4}$ or $3\frac{1}{4}$
8. $\frac{11}{10}$ or $1\frac{1}{10}$
9. $\frac{2}{5}$
10. $-\frac{4}{3}$ or $-1\frac{1}{3}$
11. $\frac{17}{21}$
12. $\frac{2}{9}$
13. $\frac{35}{3}$ or $11\frac{2}{3}$
14. $\frac{110}{13}$ or $8\frac{6}{13}$
15. $\frac{16}{15}$ or $1\frac{1}{15}$
16. $\frac{12}{77}$
17. $\frac{8}{27}$

Page 91

1. $(3, -1)$
2. $(-2, -4)$
3. infinitely many
4. 0

Page 92

1. $y = -x + 15$
2. $y = -0.5x + 10$
3.

4. $(10, 5)$
5. 10, 5

Page 93

1. $(9, 1)$
2. $(1, 3)$
3. $(2, 3)$
4. $(5, -1)$
5. $(-4, -7)$
6. $(-1, -1)$
7. $(4, 18)$
8. $(6, 20)$
9. The graph shows that the x-coordinate of the solution is negative, so Zach's solution is not reasonable.

Page 94

1. Substituting 1 for x and 3 for y in each equation results in a true statement, so Angelica's solution is correct.
2. $x + y = 20$
3. $0.50x + 0.75y = 11.50$
4. $(14, 6)$
5. 14 apples and 6 bananas

Page 95

1. 2 student tickets; 1 adult ticket
2. 4 records; 3 tapes
3. 4 local; 2 city
4. 3 pens; 3 pencils
5. 4,096 newspapers
6. 16 sandwiches, 1 container of juice; 13 sandwiches, 5 containers of juice; 10 sandwiches, 9 containers of juice; 7 sandwiches, 13 containers of juice; 4 sandwiches, 17 containers of juice; 1 sandwich, 21 containers of juice
7. 68 people

Page 96

1.

	Boys		Girls	
Tally	Frequency	Score	Frequency	Tally
II	2	36-40	1	I
I	1	31-35	1	I
II	2	26-30	2	II
I	1	21-25	2	II

Geography Test Scores		
Boys	Scores	Girls
	36-40	
	31-35	
	26-30	
	21-25	

2. 18, 15
3. 3 students
4. women
5. 18 people
6. Check graph.

Page 97

1. a
2.

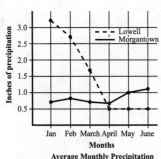

Average Monthly Precipitation

3. 4.9 inches
4. Morgantown
5. Check answer.

Page 98

1–3.

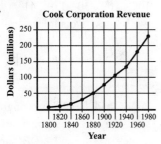

1. increasing over time
2. $40 million
3. $280 million
4. $105 million
5. $205 million
6. $83.61 million
7. Possible answer: Average income to estimate tax revenue.

Page 99

1. 57, 3, 60; 63, 27, 90; 120, 30, 150
2. 80%
3. 95%
4. Yes; the relative frequency of being a boy and playing sports is greater than the relative frequency of total students who play sports, so there is an association between being a boy and playing sports.
5. 87.5%
6. 87.5%
7. No; the relative frequency of having pets is the same for students with siblings as for the general student, so there is no association between having siblings and having pets.

Page 100

1. Possible answer: A greater number of study hours should correlate to higher test grades.
2.

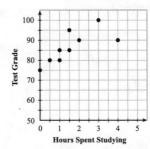

3. In general, test scores increase as the number of study hours increases.
4. No; the graph shows a general upward trend, but the grade cannot exceed 100.
5. The subject matter might be easy for a student to understand, so that student may not need to spend a lot of time studying for the test.

Page 101

1. There are clusters around the 50-minute and 80-minute intervals.
2. Possible answer: There are short wait times followed by short eruptions and longer wait times followed by longer eruptions.
3. The point near (55, 3) appears to be an outlier because it does not fall into either cluster.
4. It would not lie in either cluster because the interval is too long for the first cluster, and the duration is too short for the second cluster. It might be considered an outlier because it is not very close to the rest of the data.
5. Possible range: 3 to 5 minutes. The duration of other data points on the scatter plot that have an interval of 80 minutes is within this range.

Page 102

1. positive association, negative association, no association
2.

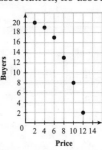

3. There is a negative association. As the price increases, the number of people who would buy the product decreases. The data appear not to be linear.

Page 103

1–2. Check graphs.
3. about 45 minutes
4. All the data points are close to the line. The data show a strong linear association, so the line should fit well.
5. No: there are two points that do not seem close to the trend line.
6. 35; Check drawings.

Page 104

1. Sample answer: (17, 170)
2. positive; linear
3. positive
4. 100, 10; 50, 5; $m = 10$
5. $b = 0$
6. $y = 10x + 0$ or $y = 10x$
7. There is an average of 10 pages per chapter; an additional chapter is associated with 10 additional pages.
8. Possible answer: Babies grow very quickly at first, but as they age, their growth rate decreases. Eventually, a person's length (height) stops increasing.

Page 105

1. $\frac{1}{8}$
2. $\frac{7}{8}$
3. $\frac{1}{4}$
4. $\frac{3}{8}$
5. $\frac{5}{8}$
6. $\frac{1}{2}$

151

7. $\frac{1}{6}$

8. $\frac{1}{3}$

9. $\frac{5}{6}$

10. $\frac{1}{2}$

11. $\frac{1}{2}$

12. 0

13. hhh, hht, hth, thh, tth, htt, tht, ttt

14. $\frac{1}{2}$

15. $\frac{1}{4}$

16. $\frac{4}{5}$

17. $\frac{8}{5}$ or $1\frac{3}{5}$

18. $\frac{7}{10}$

19. $\frac{2}{9}$

20. $\frac{4}{3}$ or $1\frac{1}{3}$

21. 35

22. 18

Page 106

1. Row 2: 2; Row 3: 3, 3; Row 4: 4, 6, 4

2. $\frac{1}{16}$

3. $\frac{1}{16}$

4. $\frac{4}{16}$ or $\frac{1}{4}$

5. $\frac{1}{32}$

6. $\frac{1}{32}$

7. $\frac{5}{32}$

8. 1, 5, 10, 10, 5, 1

9. 1, 6, 15, 20, 15, 6, 1

10. 1, 2, 4, 8, 16, 32

11. 8

12. The first and last numbers are 1. Each number in between is the sum of the two above it.

Page 107

1. 210 combinations

2. 66 ways

3. 84 ways

4. 210

5. 10! or 3,628,800

6. $2,450

7. 57 mph

8. $146\frac{2}{3}$ mi

9. $x = 27$

10. $x = 10$

11. $x = 15.2$

Page 108

1. Possible answer: about 15 spins

2. Possible answer: about 9 spins

3. 4 times

4. Possible answer: $\frac{1}{10}$

5. 5 times

6. $120

7. Check answer.

Page 109

1. $\frac{3}{5}$

2. $\frac{2}{5}$

3. 45 times

4. 10 times

5. $\frac{7}{10}$

6. 6

7. $\frac{1}{4}$

8. $\frac{13}{40}$

9. 103

10. 38.33%

Page 110

1. $\overline{AB} \approx \overline{MN}, \overline{BC} \approx \overline{NO}, \overline{CD} \approx \overline{OP}, \overline{DA} \approx \overline{PM}; \angle A \approx \angle M, \angle B \approx \angle N, \angle C \approx \angle O, \angle D \approx \angle P$

2. $a = 90°, b = 8, c = 10$

3. $a = 60°, b = 12, c = 120°$

4. $a = 75°, b = 9, c = 65°$

5. $a = 80°, b = 20, c = 15$

6. No; unless they have corresponding congruent sides as well, they are similar but not congruent.

7. ABCD is a parallelogram.

8. 16

Page 111

1. yes

2. no

3. yes

4. Check drawing.

5. A square has 4 sides of the same length; a rectangle has 2 pairs of sides of the same length.

6. No. A soccer ball is a sphere; a football has an oblong shape.

7. Check drawing.

Page 112

1. yes

2. yes

3. yes

4. $x = 20$ mm

5. $x = 1.5$ m

6. yes

7. 5

8. Possible answer: The height of the ruler is proportional to the height of the flagpole. You can use that ratio to find the distance to the flagpole.

Page 113

1–6. Check polygons.

7. 100 pieces

8. Yes. They are the same shape and one is smaller than the other.

9. Yes. They have the same shape.

Page 114

1. 109°; 109°, 30°, 139°, 41°

2. two angles, two angles, similar

3. $\overrightarrow{EF}, \overrightarrow{DF}$

4. 9, 2, 3; proportional, similar

Page 115

1. $\angle BAC$ and $\angle EDC$ are congruent since they are alternate interior angles. $\angle ABC$ and $\angle DEC$ are congruent since they are alternate interior angles. By AA similarity, $\triangle ABC$ and $\triangle DEC$ are similar.

2. 17.2 feet

3. 15

Page 116

1–2. Check drawings.

3. AE, DF

4. Check drawings.

5. $\angle DCF$, congruent; $\angle DFC$, congruent

6. $\triangle CDF$

7. AE

8. BE, CF

9. constant

Page 117

1. triangle; 120°

2. quadrilateral; 90°

3. pentagon; 72°

4. hexagon; 60°

5. octagon; 45°

6. dodecagon or 12 sided polygon; 30°

7. Any two of $\angle 1, \angle 5; \angle 2, \angle 6; \angle 4, \angle 8; \angle 3, \angle 7$

8. 120°; 5 and 6 are supplementary

152

. They would all have a measure of 90°.
10. $1\frac{7}{20}$
11. 10
12. $\frac{9}{14}$
13. $\frac{5}{19}$
14. $\frac{11}{16}$
15. $\frac{1}{5}$
16. $\frac{9}{16}$
17. $\frac{7}{15}$

Page 118

1. 1 m
2. $\frac{1}{4}$ ft
3. $\frac{1}{8}$ in.
4. 0.1 km
5. 0.5 mm
6. $\frac{1}{2}$ yd
7. 0.05 m
8. 0.005 km
9. $\frac{1}{8}$ ft
10. $\frac{1}{6}$ mi
11. 0.0005 m
12. $\frac{1}{32}$ ft
13. 49.5 mi; 50.4 mi
14. 59.5 mm; 60.4 mm
15. 34.45 km; 34.54 km
16. $11\frac{1}{4}$ yd; $11\frac{3}{4}$ yd
17. $\frac{1}{2}$ ft
18. $11\frac{1}{2}$ ft; $12\frac{1}{2}$ ft
19. Check question.

Page 119

1. 1
2. 3
3. 2
4. 30
5. 10.2
6. 10.6
7. 5
8. 8
9. 3.9
10. 4
11. 3
12. $\frac{1}{4}$
13. 7
14. $\frac{5}{3}$
15. $\frac{8}{6}$
16. 4.6
17. 2
18. 4.684

Page 120

1. πrs, where s is the slant height of the cone
2. 2, 2, h
3. 75.36 cm^2
4. 65.9 cm^2
5. 314 cm^2
6. 125.6 cm^2
7. 35.3 cm^2
8. 235.5 cm^2
9. 207.2 cm^2
10. 205.0 cm^2
11. 21.1 cm^2
12. 62.8 cm^2
13. 62.1 cm^2
14. 33.5 cm^2
15. 115.4 cm^2
16. 3.141593

Page 121

1. 65 m^3
2. 339 ft^3
3. 49 in.^{3}
4. 13 in.^{3}
5. 4,974 ft^3
6. 6 m^3
7. 37.68 m^3
8. 8 m
9. 61.4 cm^2
10. 45.8 cm^2

Page 122

1. 9,231.6 ft^3
2. 395.64 m^3
3. 57,697.5 ft^3
4. 4 times, or 9,231.6 cm^3
5. 35.33 in.^{3}
6. 69.08 in.^{3}
7. 3 cm
8. 7 m

Page 123

1. 39 tennis balls
2. 381.51 g
3. 102.96 in.^{3}
4. 51 oranges
5. 1 hour
6. $537.50
7. $2.84
8. about 24 min 30 sec
9. 5 trips

Page 124

1. $a = 180 - (72 + 65)$; 43°
2. $a = 180 - (65 + 35)$; 80°
3. 71°
4. 30°
5. 88°, 29°, 63°
6. 90°, 45°, 45°
7. 4^5
8. 10^3
9. 8^3
10. 4^{-4} or $\left(\frac{1}{4}\right)^4$

Page 125

1. 40°, 76°, 64°
2. 129°, 19°, 161°
3. 117°
4. 79°
5. 90°
6. 120°

Page 126

1. $\angle 2 + \angle 3$
2. $\angle 1 + \angle 3$
3. $\angle 1 + \angle 2$
4. 65°
5. 120°
6. 80°
7. 115°
8. 65°
9. 76°
10. 80°
11. 360°
12. The sum of the measures of the exterior angles of a triangle is 360°.

Page 127

1–2. Check drawings.
3. c^2 square units
4. Check drawings.
5. a^2 square units; b^2 square units
6. $a^2 + b^2$ square units
7. Yes, the outlines of the figures are the same size.
8. Yes; the shaded regions have the same area. (They are made of congruent triangles and the total area of the figures is equal.) Subtracting the shaded region from the total area gives the same area for the unshaded region in each figure.
9. $a^2 + b^2 = c^2$

153

Page 128

1. yes, yes, yes, yes, yes
2. Check figures.
3. Check figures. yes, yes, yes, yes, yes
4. Students should note that each set of lengths satisfies the equation $a^2 + b^2 = c^2$ and should have successfully made a right triangle with the strips of grid paper. They should conclude that the converse of the Pythagorean Theorem is true.

Page 129

1. hypotenuse: $\overline{BC}$; legs: $\overline{AC}, \overline{AB}$
2. hypotenuse: $\overline{DE}$; legs: $\overline{DF}, \overline{EF}$
3. hypotenuse: $\overline{GI}$; legs: $\overline{HI}, \overline{HG}$
4. hypotenuse: $\overline{BC}$; legs: $\overline{AB}, \overline{AC}$
5. hypotenuse: $\overline{DF}$; legs: $\overline{DE}, \overline{EF}$
6. hypotenuse: $\overline{GI}$; legs: $\overline{HI}, \overline{GH}$
7. no
8. yes
9. yes
10. no
11. yes
12. no
13. 720
14. 362,880
15. 479,001,600
16. 1,680
17. 30,240

Page 130

1–3. Check drawings.
1. yes
2. no
3. yes
4. no; 7^2, 8^2, 16, 49, 64, 65 $\neq$ 64
5. yes; 5^2, 12^2, 25, 144, 169, 169 = 169
6. no; 5^2, 9^2, 25, 36, 81, 61 $\neq$ 81
7. yes; 16^2, 20^2, 144, 256, 400, 400 = 400
8. yes
9. no
10. yes
11. One possible answer: 8 and 6; 36 + 64 = 100 = 4(25). It is a multiple of 25.

Page 131

1. 12.8 in.
2. 21.2 m
3. 13 m
4. 10.8 cm
5. 17 in.
6. no; $15^2 + 15^2 \neq 20^2$
7. yes; $15^2 + 36^2 = 39^2$
8. $\sqrt{89} \approx 9.4$ ft
9. 45 sq ft
10. 6 fish
11. 130 ft; 300 ft

Page 132

1. 30 ft
2. 24 ft
3. $c = 10$
4. $b = 12$
5. $a = 15$
6. $b = 4$
7. $a = 7$
8. $c = 17$
9. $c = 20$
10. $b = 12$
11. No; the length of the leg can be substituted for either a or b since both a and b represent the lengths of the legs.
12. No the square root of a whole number is not always a whole number

Page 133

1. $a = 5$ m
2. $b = 5.7$ mm
3. $a = 5.4$ m
4. $c = 2.2$ mm
5. 16.2 m
6. 62.6 m
7. 33.5 m
8. 46.6 ft
9. 10 yrs old
10. 35 ft; Check problem.

Page 134

1. 17 ft
2. 36 m
3. 11.5 in.
4. 8.9 cm
5. $\sqrt{145}$ ft
6. 12.21 ft
7. 12 ft

Page 135

1–5. Answers may vary.
1. 7.1 units
2. 8.1 units
3. 5.8 units
4. 6.4 units
5. Estimate: between 10 and 10.5; Actual: 10.296 units

Page 136

1. $5\sqrt{2}$
2. $7\sqrt{2}$
3. $\frac{(3\sqrt{2})}{2}$
4. $6\sqrt{2}$
5. 3
6. $2\sqrt{3}$
7. $5\sqrt{3}$
8. 18
9. about 14.2 ft
10. $45\sqrt{2}$ ft or 63.6 ft
11. -9
12. -14
13. -12
14. 36
15. -42
16. 5
17. 16
18. 0

Page 137

1. $d = 4$
2. $d = 7$
3. $d = 7$
4. $d = 5$
5. $d = 13$
6. $d = 15$
7. $d = 10$
8. $d = 13$
9. $d = 5$
10. $d = 9.4$
11. $d = 7$
12. $d = 1.4$

154